fem·i·nism

fem·i·nism

A Brief Introduction to the Ideas,
Debates, and Politics of the Movement

DEBORAH CAMERON

The University of Chicago Press

The University of Chicago Press, Chicago 60637
© 2019 by Deborah Cameron
All rights reserved. No part of this book may be used or reproduced in any
manner whatsoever without written permission, except in the case of brief
quotations in critical articles and reviews. For more information, contact
the University of Chicago Press, 1427 E. 60th St., Chicago, IL 60637.
Published 2019
Printed in the United States of America

28 27 26 25 24 23 22 21 20 19   1 2 3 4 5

ISBN-13: 978-0-226-62059-6 (cloth)
ISBN-13: 978-0-226-62062-6 (paper)
ISBN-13: 978-0-226-62076-3 (e-book)
DOI: https://doi.org/10.7208/chicago/9780226620763.001.0001

First published in Great Britain in 2018 by Profile Books Ltd.
© Deborah Cameron 2018

Library of Congress Cataloging-in-Publication Data

Names: Cameron, Deborah, 1958– author.
Title: Feminism : a brief introduction to the ideas, debates, and politics of the
    movement / Deborah Cameron.
Description: Chicago : The University of Chicago Press, 2019. | Includes
    bibliographical references and index.
Identifiers: LCCN 2018042176 | ISBN 9780226620596 (cloth : alk. paper) |
    ISBN 9780226620626 (pbk. : alk. paper) | ISBN 9780226620763 (e-book)
Subjects: LCSH: Feminism. | Women—Social conditions.
Classification: LCC HQ1206 .C24 2019 | DDC 305.42—dc23
LC record available at https://lccn.loc.gov/2018042176

♾ This paper meets the requirements of ANSI/NISO Z39.48-1992
(Permanence of Paper).

Contents

Acknowledgments

I am grateful to all the feminists whose collective wisdom I have learned from over the years. Thanks to Marina Strinkovsky, Teresa Baron, and Nancy Hawker, and special thanks to my best critic, Meryl Altman.

Introduction:
What Is Feminism?

"We should all be feminists," declared the writer Chimamanda Ngozi Adichie in her 2014 essay of that name.[1] But an *Economist*/YouGov poll conducted in the same year found that many Americans were not so sure. Only one in four of those surveyed said they would describe themselves as feminists, and another one in four considered "feminist" an insult.[2]

Ambivalence about feminism is nothing new. In 1938 the British writer Dorothy L. Sayers gave a lecture to a women's society entitled "Are Women Human?" She began with this disclaimer: "Your Secretary made the suggestion that she thought I must be interested in the feminist movement. I replied—a little irritably, I am afraid—that I was not sure I wanted to 'identify myself,' as the phrase goes, with feminism. . . ."[3] This sentiment was common enough in the 1930s and 1940s to prompt a contemporary of Sayers, the novelist Winifred Holtby, to ask, "Why are women themselves so often the first to repudiate the movements of the past hundred and fifty years, which gained for them at least the foundations of political, economic, educational and moral equality?"[4]

One answer might be that many women are wary of the *word* "feminist," which has a long history of being used to disparage those so labeled as dour, unfeminine man-haters. But people who reject the label may nevertheless hold views that could be described as feminist. Some respondents to the 2014 poll mentioned above changed their initial, negative answer to the question, "Do you consider yourself to be a feminist?" after they were given a definition of a feminist as "someone who believes in the social, political and economic equality of the sexes." Attitudes toward feminism tend to vary depending on what the term is being used to talk about. When people use the word "feminism," they may be referring to any or all of the following things:

- An idea: as Marie Shear once put it, "the radical notion that women are people."[5]

- A collective political project: in the words of bell hooks, "a movement to end sexism, sexist exploitation and oppression."[6]

- An intellectual framework: what the philosopher Nancy Hartsock described as "a mode of analysis . . . a way of asking questions and searching for answers."[7]

These different senses have different histories, and the way they fit together is complicated.

Feminism as an idea is much older than the political movement. The beginnings of political feminism are usually located in the late eighteenth century, but a tradition of writing in which women defended their sex against unjust vilification had existed for several centuries before that. The text that inaugurated this tradition was Christine de Pizan's *Book of the City of Ladies*.[8] Written by an educated secular woman in France at the beginning of the fifteenth century, this book was a systematic attempt to rebut the misogynistic arguments male authorities had made about women: it argued that a person's worth should be judged not by their sex but by their character and their conduct.

Over the next four hundred years, other texts making similar arguments appeared in various parts of Europe. Their authors were relatively few in number, were not part of any collective movement, and did not call themselves feminists (that word did not come into use until the nineteenth century). But they clearly subscribed to "the radical notion that women are people." Because their writings criticized the masculinist bias of what passed for knowledge about women in their time, they have sometimes been described as the first feminist theorists.

Dorothy Sayers also believed that women were people. "A woman," she wrote, "is just as much an ordinary human being as a man, with the same individual preferences, and with just as much right to the tastes and preferences of an individual." But that belief was what made Sayers reluctant to embrace feminism as an organized political movement. "What is repugnant to every human being," she went on, "is to be reckoned always as a member of a class and not as an individual person." This is the paradox at the heart of feminism in the second, "political movement" sense: to assert that they are people, just as men are, women must unite on the basis of being women. And since women are a very large, internally diverse group, it has always been difficult to unite them. Feminists may be united in their support for abstract ideals like freedom, equality, and justice, but they have rarely agreed about what those ideals mean in concrete reality. Feminism as a political movement has only ever commanded mass support when its goals were compatible with a range of beliefs and interests.

The movement for women's voting rights, which began in the nineteenth century and peaked in the early twentieth, is a case in point. Two of the central arguments deployed by suffrage campaigners rested on different, and theoretically opposed, beliefs about the nature and social role of women. One view emphasized women's similarity to men in order to argue that they deserved the same political rights, while the other emphasized women's difference from men, arguing that women's distinctive concerns could not be adequately represented by an all-male electorate. (These two positions are sometimes described in shorthand as equality feminism and difference feminism.) The movement's objective—gaining political representation for women—also brought together people whose other interests and allegiances were not just different, but in some cases directly opposed. In the United States there were Black women whose support for the cause reflected the belief that women's enfranchisement would advance the struggle for racial justice; conversely, there were white feminists who courted southern segregationists using the racist argument that enfranchising white women would bolster white supremacy.[9] Upper-class feminists sometimes argued that educated, property-owning women had a better claim to the vote than working-class men; socialists by contrast favored enfranchising all women, as well as all men, since that would strengthen the position of the working class as a whole. Many disparate interest groups stood to benefit from the extension of voting rights to women, and that was enough to bring them into an alliance. But once the vote had been won, women's differences reasserted themselves and solidarity gave way to conflict.

Feminism's story is not a linear narrative of continuous progress. The movement keeps being reinvented, partly to meet the challenges of new times, but also because of each new generation's desire to differentiate itself from the one before. Holtby's complaint about women's repudiating the movement was made at a time when many younger women were questioning the need for feminism in a postsuffrage world: they saw both the cause and the women who had fought for it as relics of the past, with little relevance to their concerns. Something similar would happen fifty years later, as young women in the 1980s and 1990s rejected their mothers' "Women's Lib" and media pundits proclaimed the advent of a postfeminist era. But those commentators spoke too soon: today the movement is on the march again (literally: witness the size and scale of the women's marches held to protest the inauguration of President Donald Trump in 2017), and according to polls like the one I mentioned earlier, the women currently most likely to identify themselves as feminists are those under the age of thirty. Their version of feminism has continuities with earlier versions, but it is also distinctive, reflecting the conditions and the ideas of its time.

The interplay of continuity and change is emphasized in one common way of organizing historical accounts of feminism—through the idea that it has advanced in a series of waves. According to this account, the first wave began when women came together to demand legal and civil rights in the mid-nineteenth century and ended with the victory of the suffrage campaign in the 1920s. The upsurge of feminist activism that began in the late 1960s was labeled the second wave by activists who wanted to stress the continuity between their own movement and the more radical elements of nineteenth-century feminism. A third wave was proclaimed by a new generation of activists in the early 1990s, who explicitly contrasted their approach with that of the second wave. The renewed interest in feminism that has become visible in the past ten years is sometimes described as a fourth wave.

The wave model, though widely used, has prompted numerous criticisms. One is that it oversimplifies history by suggesting that each new wave supersedes the previous one, when in fact the legacy of past waves remains visible in the present. Many second-wave creations (like women's studies courses and shelters for women escaping domestic violence) are still part of the contemporary feminist landscape; some feminist organizations that remain active today have their roots in the struggles of the first wave (they include Planned Parenthood, founded in 1916, and the League of Women Voters, created in 1920 to promote civic and political engagement among the newly enfranchised female population). The wave model has also been criticized for overgeneralizing the feminism of each historical moment, as though all the women who came of age politically in the 1960s, or in the 1990s, shared the same beliefs and concerns. In reality they did not: political differences and disagreements, like the ones mentioned earlier within the suffrage movement, have existed in every wave and among women of every generation. A third objection is that the discontinuity of a wave narrative obscures the actual continuity of feminist activism, which didn't just stop in the 1920s and lie dormant until the late 1960s. The suffrage campaign ended when its objective was achieved, but campaigns to advance women's rights continued in other forms and other venues.

This last observation points to a more general difficulty in writing the history of feminism as a political movement: it is, and always has been, decentralized and somewhat amorphous. Its history concerns not just specifically feminist organizations but also other organizations in which feminist goals have been pursued—for instance, organizations affiliated with the labor movement, the peace movement, the environmentalist movement, and various movements for racial justice.[10] Autonomous feminist movements, organized by women and for women, have often developed out of other political struggles, like the French Revolution in the late eighteenth century, the abolitionist movement in the nineteenth century, and the civil rights, antiwar, and anticolonialist movements of the twentieth century. Led by their involvement in these campaigns to see their own situation as oppressive, some women broke away to form their own feminist organizations. Others chose to stay where they were, but that does not mean they were not also feminists.

If we consider feminism in the third sense—as an intellectual framework—the picture is not much more straightforward. Feminism does not match our usual prototype for a philosophical movement or theoretical current, such as existentialism or poststructuralism, because it does not center on the works of an agreed canon of Great Thinkers. Some theoretical texts are widely acknowledged as foundational in the history of modern feminist thought, like Mary Wollstonecraft's *A Vindication of the Rights of Woman* (1792) and Simone de Beauvoir's *The Second Sex* (originally published in French in 1949), but beyond that it would be hard to make a list that every feminist would agree on.[11] "Feminism" is a label that often comes with a modifier, such as "Black," "socialist," "liberal," "radical," or "intersectional." Some of the categories overlap—an individual feminist can claim allegiance to several at once—while others are, or are seen as, opposed. On some issues there is relatively little disagreement among feminists, but on others the differences can be stark.

So far, then, my answer to the question, What is feminism?, could be summed up by saying, "It's complicated." Feminism is multifaceted, diverse in both its historical forms and in its political and intellectual content: it's an umbrella sheltering beliefs and interests that may be not just different but incompatible with one another. (And some of those beliefs are also held by people who deny they are feminists at all.) Is there anything that holds it all together, any set of basic principles to which all self-identified feminists subscribe? Many writers have concluded that the answer is no, and that we should speak not of feminism in the singular but of feminisms, plural. Attempts to generalize usually produce definitions that are too general to be useful: for instance, defining feminism as an active desire to change women's position in society immediately invites the question, Change it from what to what? It might also invite the criticism that in the twenty-first century overtly *anti*feminist groups also manifest an active desire to change women's position in society. Other common definitions, like the one used by the YouGov pollsters (feminism is a belief in the social, political and economic equality of the sexes), are open to the criticism that they equate feminism in general with a particular (Western liberal) feminist tradition; as we will see in chapter 2, many feminists have questioned, or even rejected, the idea that feminism is all about equality.

In this book I aim to reflect and explore the complexity of feminism(s), but since we need to start somewhere, I will start by offering a minimal definition. Feminism undoubtedly comes in many different varieties, but all of them, arguably, rest on two fundamental beliefs:

1. That women occupy a subordinate position in society and suffer certain injustices and systemic disadvantages because they are women.

2. That the subordination of women is neither inevitable nor desirable: it can and should be changed through political action.

Feminists differ on the reasons why women occupy a subordinate position in society, how their subordination is maintained, who benefits from it, and what its consequences are, but they all agree that women's subordination is real and that it has existed in some form in the majority of the human societies for which we have any record. Antifeminists, by contrast, may deny that women are subordinated: some supporters of the contemporary men's rights movement claim that women in modern Western societies have become the dominant sex and that it is men who are now oppressed. Other antifeminist ideologies acknowledge the subordinate status of women but justify it by asserting that it is ordained by God or nature. Rejecting such justifications is another fundamental feminist principle. Though feminists may disagree on what changes they want to see in the position of women, all believe that change is necessary, and all assume that it is possible.

Although I have been using the generic term "women," this usage should not be taken to imply that women are an internally homogeneous group who all suffer the same injustices and disadvantages. Most currents of contemporary feminism incorporate the principle that Kimberlé Crenshaw labels "intersectionality," which acknowledges that women's experiences are varied, shaped not only by their sex but also by other aspects of their identity and social positioning such as race, ethnicity, sexuality, and social class.[12] Different systems of dominance and subordination, such as sexism and racism, intersect to produce different outcomes for different groups of women and, not infrequently, conflicts of interest between them.

As well as thinking about the relationships among differently situated women within one society, we also have to consider the situations of women across national and regional boundaries: we live in a globalized world, and feminism today is a global movement. Some currents within feminism (communist ones, for instance, and those associated with anticolonialist struggles) have always had a strongly internationalist outlook. But more recent developments have enabled new ways of thinking, and acting, globally. In her preface to the 2015 edition of *This Bridge Called My Back*, a classic collection of writings by women of color in the United States, Cherríe Moraga points out that the first edition of the book, published in 1981, predated the internet, mobile phones, and twenty-four-hour news channels. Although most contributors were linked by ancestry and history to places beyond the United States and were conscious of the interconnectedness of women's struggles around the world, geographical distance still made a difference: "Egypt, Afghanistan, Nigeria all seemed very far away."[13] Now, in the age of global communications, it has become easier to organize politically in ways that transcend what Moraga calls "the barriers of state-imposed nationality," and many feminist campaigns have a global dimension that they might have lacked in the past.

One high-profile example is the #MeToo movement, which had its roots in a local initiative started in 2006 by Bronx-based community activist Tarana Burke. In 2017, following a series of well-publicized revelations about sexual harassment and abuse in Hollywood, another woman, Alyssa Milano, put a call out on Twitter for more women to share their experiences using the hashtag #MeToo. This was intended as both a gesture of solidarity with the women who had named their abusers publicly and a strategy for demonstrating the scale of the problem, which is not confined to a single industry or a single country. On Twitter, the call was soon taken up by women located outside the United States. #MeToo subsequently became a global phenomenon with many local manifestations.

Another, somewhat different example is the transnational response to the collapse of the Rana Plaza garment factory in Bangladesh in 2013, a disaster in which more than eleven hundred workers—most of them women—died and twenty-five hundred more were injured. Activists resisted attempts to present this as a purely local tragedy, pointing out that the factory was part of a global supply chain producing clothing for first-world fashion retailers. In an age when capitalism is organized globally, effective campaigns for the rights of workers must also adopt a global approach. So, while campaigners in Dhaka demanded that the local owner and managers face the consequences of their negligence, campaigners in the United States and Europe held retailers to account and pressed them to adopt new policies on workers' safety and conditions of employment.

The global nature of contemporary feminism will be explored in the following chapters, but women's struggles in different parts of the world have distinct as well as shared features, and a book as short as this cannot do justice to all the local or regional traditions of feminist thinking and political activism that would need to be represented in a truly global account.[14] I should acknowledge, therefore, that my main focus will be on the Western—and especially the Anglo-American—feminism of the twentieth and twenty-first centuries. This is itself an internally diverse tradition, and one that has become increasingly aware of the need to think globally. But it is certainly not the only tradition, and in making it my main reference point (a choice that reflects my own location), I am not suggesting that it is or should be the main reference point for all feminists everywhere.

The story of feminism is full of complications. The label "feminist" has never been actively embraced by all women or even the majority of women, and there have always been differences and conflicts among the women who did embrace it. Yet feminism has survived; reports of its death have always turned out to be exaggerated. Its core idea— "the radical notion that women are people"—is one that few people today would openly dissent from. But the devil is in the detail of what follows from the idea in practice. The answers feminists have given to that question are the subject of the rest of this book.

1

Domination

Naomi Alderman's 2016 novel *The Power* imagines a future world where women are the dominant sex, and where it is generally assumed they always have been.[1] The main narrative purports to be the work of a male writer who wants to challenge orthodox assumptions by telling the story of a time in the distant past when women overthrew the rule of men. The revolution began when girls discovered they could generate electricity in their own bodies and use it to deliver painful or even fatal electric shocks. At first they used this power mainly in self-defense; then they began to exploit it, and men's fear of it, for their own advantage. Soon women were running everything from national governments to organized crime. They became sexually aggressive and sometimes abused men for their own pleasure. They created new myths that made their dominance appear natural; in time, the very idea that men had once had power would be dismissed as absurd, the product of idle speculation and wishful thinking.

Alderman has said of her book that it is only a dystopia if you're male: what happens to men in her imagined world is no worse than what women endure in the real one. But *The Power* doesn't fit the usual template for a feminist utopia either. The ideal societies of feminist speculative fiction, from Charlotte Perkins Gilman's *Herland* (1915) to Marge Piercy's *Woman on the Edge of Time* (1976), are generally egalitarian places where women live (either with or without men) in peace and harmony with nature.[2] The world of *The Power* is more like our world, except that women and men have swapped places. The novel invites us to ask whether women, if they had power over men, would abuse it in the same ways men have abused their power over women. But as we ponder this hypothetical question, we are bound to wonder why, in reality, women *don't* have power over men. Wherever one sex dominates the other, it is invariably men who dominate women. To us, this seems as self-evident as its opposite does in Alderman's fictional far-off future. Has there ever been a society in which women dominated men? Outside fiction and mythology, could such a society exist?

These questions have been debated, by feminists and others, for well over a century. In this chapter I consider some of the arguments writers have put forward about the origins of male dominance, how its forms have changed over time, and what keeps it in place today. First, though, I should clarify what is—and what is not—meant by describing a society as "male dominated."

General statements about male dominance are often met with the "not all men" objection: feminists are asked how they justify blaming men in general for things that only some men do. Alternatively, they may be accused of glossing over the existence of women who do equally terrible things. So it's important to clarify that when feminists talk about male dominance, or patriarchy (a term that literally means "the rule of the father" but in feminist usage is more commonly a synonym for male dominance), they are not making a claim primarily about the attitudes, intentions, or behavior of individual men. Rather, it's a claim about social structures. A male-dominated or patriarchal society is one whose structures and institutions—legal, political, religious, economic—put men in a position of power over women.

It is true, of course, that individual men may choose to forgo certain rights and privileges. A notable historical example is Henry Browne Blackwell, one of the founders of the Republican Party and an active supporter of women's suffrage. When he married the abolitionist and feminist Lucy Stone in Massachusetts in 1855, Blackwell promised that he would make no use of the rights the law gave husbands over the bodies, property, and earnings of their wives.[3] A copy of this pledge was published in a newspaper, and other couples subsequently incorporated similar statements in their own wedding ceremonies. But the principled stand taken by Blackwell and others did not make men's collective dominance disappear, just as an individual boss's commitment to treating his workers well does not change the fact that capitalism is a system based on exploitation. His promise was not legally binding: he remained free to retract it, and the authorities did not have to respect it, as he and Stone later discovered when they tried to register property in her birth name. Her status as an equal partner in the marriage thus depended entirely on how her husband chose to treat her. Real equality is about structures, not the personal morality of individuals.

What does structural male dominance look like? The short answer is that it varies: it is neither uniform across cultures nor static and unchanging over time. That said, a male-dominated society will likely exhibit some or all of the following characteristics:

· Men monopolize or dominate positions of political power and leadership, and have more say in political decision-making than women.

· Men have rights under the law that women do not.

· Men own or control more economic resources than women.

· Men have direct authority—sanctioned by law, religion, and custom—over women in their family or household.

· Men use violence and the threat of it to control and intimidate women.

· Men's activities, occupations, cultural products, and ideas or forms of knowledge are accorded higher status than women's.

Different societies exhibit these characteristics in different ways and to differing degrees, and the profile of a single society may change significantly over time. Whereas the United States in Lucy Stone's time had all the characteristics listed above, American society today looks very different. Married men no longer have direct, legally sanctioned authority over their wives; women are equal to men in law and have gained full political representation. Yet it is still true, not only in the United States but around the world, that men occupy most positions of power and leadership, that they control more economic resources, and that male violence against women remains endemic. It should also be acknowledged that improvements in women's overall position since the nineteenth century have not benefited all women equally. There are clear differences between women of different generations, classes, and ethnic groups, between more- and less-educated women, and between women who have children and those who don't.

Differences also exist among men, and that raises another question about what we mean by calling a society male dominated. Do we mean that *all* men have more power, wealth, freedom, and status than *all* women? The short answer to that question is no. In societies that are stratified by caste, class, race, or ethnicity, many men will be excluded from political and economic power, and women in a higher social stratum will have authority over men from a lower one. The slaveholder's wife could give orders to male slaves; the feudal lady of the manor had higher status than the male agricultural workers on her husband's estate. But even the highest-ranking woman in feudal or plantation society was still required to submit to the authority of her husband. The same principle applied at other levels of the social hierarchy. The agricultural worker, for instance, was obliged to defer to his master's wife, but at home he could expect his own wife to defer to him.

The relevance of this point—essentially, that the same inequality between men and women is reproduced at every level of the social structure—is sometimes lost in discussions of the differences and inequalities among women. If a Hollywood megastar complains that her male costar got paid twice as much as she did for their last film, some feminists will immediately suggest that she should check her privilege, pointing out that millions of women's lives would be transformed by even a tiny fraction of her enormous earnings. And of course, that is a legitimate point. I'm certainly not going to argue that fighting for gender parity among millionaires should be a feminist political priority. But it doesn't mean that the existence of a gender pay gap among Hollywood A-listers (or CEOs, or bankers) is of no interest to feminists at all. It's another piece of evidence that male dominance is *structural*: it pervades the system from top to bottom. We may (indeed, we should) care more about its effects on women at the bottom, but what ultimately has to be dismantled is the whole edifice. This is why many feminists argue for retaining some general concept of male dominance, or patriarchy, while also paying attention to the differences among women.

But I still haven't answered the question I raised at the beginning of this chapter: how common is male dominance itself? Is it found in all societies past and present, or have there been exceptions—societies where neither sex dominates, or where women dominate men? Many (though not all) feminists would say that egalitarian societies, where neither sex dominates, do exist but female-dominated societies do not. There have been societies whose rulers were women, including some where a female despot or absolute monarch (like Catherine the Great of Russia) had enormous power over subjects of both sexes. However, a despotism in which the despot may be female is not the same thing as a structurally female-dominated society. Of the latter, the historical record provides no clear examples. Which raises the question, how do we explain their absence?

One traditional explanation relies on a form of biological determinism: male dominance is the inevitable consequence of the natural differences between the sexes. Men dominate women rather than vice versa because men are bigger, stronger, and more aggressive, and because they are less constrained by their role in human reproduction. In its basic form, this argument is often presented as simple common sense, but it also comes in more elaborate, scientific versions. Evolutionary theorists have regularly argued that male dominance, or the traits that underpin it like aggressiveness and competitiveness, evolved to serve the interest of both sexes in passing on their genes to offspring. Women, who must invest more time and energy in reproduction, can maximize their reproductive success by exchanging sex—and its products, children carrying both parents' genes—for men's services as providers and protectors. Their natural role is not to dominate but to nurture.

This is not an argument favored by most feminists, since it implies that male dominance and female subordination are inescapable facts of nature. Feminism requires the belief that our social arrangements can be changed. Commitment to that proposition has led many feminists, and other opponents of biological determinism, to ponder the historical origins of patriarchy. If patriarchy can be shown to have a history—if we can say when, where, how, and why it originated—then we do not have to accept it as part of the human condition: something was there before it, and something could be put in its place.

Reconstructing the origins of patriarchy is not a straightforward task, because the evidence (especially about the lives of our preliterate ancestors) is both limited and difficult to interpret. Nevertheless, various scholars have attempted it, drawing on the evidence provided by archaeology, anthropology, and ancient history and the study of mythology. The earliest accounts were produced in the nineteenth century by men like the Swiss scholar Johann Jakob Bachofen and the American anthropologist Lewis Henry Morgan, who had spent time living among the Iroquois Indians. Both argued that patriarchy had displaced an earlier form of social organization that was matriarchal, in the literal sense of "ruled by mothers." Early human societies were imagined to have practiced unregulated sexual promiscuity, or group marriage, which made it impossible to establish the paternity of children. These societies were therefore matrilineal (they traced descent through the female line), and the basic unit of society was the female-headed clan, centered on a group of sisters and their children. Patriarchy resulted from a shift to patrilineal descent. Under this system sisters were separated, each going to live with her husband's clan, to which her children would also belong.

On the question why the hypothetical shift from matriarchy to patriarchy occurred, perhaps the most influential early account was the one offered by Friedrich Engels in his 1884 book *The Origin of the Family, Private Property, and the State*. Engels placed earlier scholarship within the framework of historical materialism, the Marxist approach that holds that "the determining factor in history is . . . the production and reproduction of the immediate essentials of life," which encompasses both "the production of the means of existence, of articles of food and clothing, dwellings, and of the tools necessary for that production" and "the production of human beings themselves, the propagation of the species." In any given time and place, the overall character of society would reflect both the way labor was organized and the way families were structured. In Engels's account, the emergence of the patriarchal family followed from a change in "the production of the means of existence," namely the development of pastoralism (the breeding and herding of domesticated animals). This advancement increased the wealth of the clan while also giving its men, who were usually responsible for tending livestock, a more important role. The men exploited their new position to ensure that they would be able to pass their property on to their own children. This goal required the replacement of the traditional system based on what Bachofen had dubbed "mother-right" with one based on father-right. Engels famously described the imposition of this system as "the world historical defeat of the female sex." As a result of it, he wrote, "the woman was degraded and reduced to servitude[;] she became the slave of [the man's] lust and a mere instrument for the production of children."[4]

In her 1986 book *The Creation of Patriarchy*, the feminist historian Gerda Lerner presented a slightly different account. She agreed with Engels that the emergence of patriarchy was connected to new developments in the mode of production (farming), but she disputed his argument that women were subjugated because of men's wish to secure the passage of their property to their own descendants. Rather, she argued that men turned women themselves, along with their children, *into* property as a way to meet the increased demand for human labor that new modes of production created. Increasing the available labor power required communities to produce more children, which in turn required greater numbers of fertile women; this need could be satisfied by capturing and enslaving women from neighboring groups.[5]

Other feminists in the 1970s and 1980s tried to show that male dominance was not the inevitable product of biological sex differences, by pointing to present-day societies that were not organized on patriarchal principles. The societies they took as exemplars, though sometimes labeled "matriarchal," were not female dominated; rather they were—or were said to be—egalitarian. Whether they really warranted that description was a subject of some debate among feminist anthropologists.[6] Some argued that male dominance really is universal, pointing out that even in supposedly egalitarian societies it is men who dominate high-status public or ritual functions. Among the matrilineal Iroquois, for instance, women are clan mothers but only men serve as tribal chiefs. Others maintained that although there was usually a division of roles between men and women— they were not equal in the sense of being identical and interchangeable—their roles and the products of their labor were valued equally, and neither sex was exploited or controlled by the other.

Some of the clearest surviving cases of egalitarianism are the hunter-gatherer societies that have maintained their traditional way of life. Studies suggest that men and women in these societies typically contribute equally to the survival of the community, play an equal part in decision-making, and enjoy similar levels of personal and sexual freedom. In some cases there is little or no difference in their day-to-day activities (it is not true that women never hunt or fish and that men never gather). Hunter-gatherers are not just egalitarian in the negative sense of not having developed hierarchies: they cultivate an ethos of cooperation and sharing and firmly discourage displays of individual dominance. Against the argument that male dominance is a product of natural selection, some researchers have suggested that its absence may actually have been advantageous for early humans.[7]

But while the existence of egalitarian societies shows that male dominance is not a universal fact of nature, the examples described in the anthropological literature do not offer a very helpful model for feminists living in complex modern societies. It's true that they have inspired both fictional feminist utopias (Mattapoisett, the egalitarian society in Marge Piercy's novel *Woman on the Edge of Time*, is a technologically enhanced version of the culture of the matrilineal Wampanoag Indians) and some real-life experiments with alternative ways of living. But we can't all go back to foraging or horticulturalism, and few of us would want to. The goal of most feminists is to lessen, and ultimately eliminate, male dominance as it exists in the conditions of the twenty-first century. For that purpose it might be less important to probe the origins of patriarchy and more important to analyze its current forms—which have clearly changed, not just since the dawn of civilization, but since the 1880s when Engels was writing, and even since the feminist debates of the 1970s and 1980s.

In her book *Theorizing Patriarchy*, Sylvia Walby suggests that during the past century there has been a grad-

ual shift from "private" to more "public" forms of patriarchy.[8] What she means by private patriarchy is a system in
which women are dominated by individual men—husbands,
fathers, brothers—within the private sphere of the home and
family. This was what male dominance looked like to Engels
in the 1880s: the law gave married men near-absolute power
over their wives, and for most women there was no alternative to marriage since they were barred from or unqualified
for the kinds of paid work that would have enabled them to
support themselves. This private form of male dominance
cannot be said to have disappeared entirely, for some communities in the United States—including certain fundamentalist Christian ones—still maintain their belief in the submission of wives to husbands. But that norm no longer has
the backing of the law and other secular institutions. Marriage itself is now something most women have a choice
about, and their choices are no longer dictated by a system that denies women education or employment simply
because they are women.

This shift does not mean, however, that women are no
longer subordinated in any way. Rather, it means that they
experience their subordinate status less in their private
relationships with individual men and more in their public
roles as citizens and employees. In the sphere of work, for
instance (discussed further in chapter 3), women are still
concentrated in low-paid and low-status occupations, are
subject to sex discrimination, and are disadvantaged by the
expectation that they will also be responsible for unpaid care
work at home. Since the 1990s, austerity programs that have
scaled back public services have had a particularly negative
effect on women, both because the services in question are
major employers of women and because their withdrawal
increases the amount of unpaid care work women must do.

Sex is another domain in which Walby suggests a shift

has occurred in the form male dominance typically takes. The past fifty years are often thought of as an era of sexual liberation: since the 1960s, sexual minorities have gained greater social acceptance, and the stigma attached to sex outside marriage has decreased. The risk of unwanted pregnancy has been reduced by access to reliable contraception, and it is no longer assumed that "normal" women are uninterested in sex. But while in many ways these developments have been positive for both sexes, feminists have questioned the idea that women now have the same sexual freedom as men (this is a subject I'll return to in chapter 5). Here too, arguably, there has been a shift from private patriarchy—a system in which women are defined as the exclusive sexual property of their husbands—to a more public form in which it is assumed that women are or should be sexually available to any man. What used to be forbidden to women and girls is now expected of them, and all too often it is forced on them. This form of male dominance, whether manifested in the phenomenon of "rape culture" on college campuses, workplace sexual harassment, or presidential boasts about "grabbing [women] by the pussy," is central to the maintenance of modern patriarchal power, and as such has become an increasingly visible focus for feminist campaigns like #MeToo and Time's Up.

As we saw earlier, virtually all accounts of the origins of patriarchy suggest that a significant factor in its emergence was the desire of men to exploit and control women's reproductive capacities. Some feminists have argued that for millennia women were unable to resist male dominance precisely because they were, to quote Shulamith Firestone, "at the continual mercy of their biology." But by the time Firestone was writing, in 1970, advances in science and technology had changed this. She even suggested that artificial reproduction could someday be used to free women from their biological burden entirely. This proposal was never widely accepted among feminists, but most were in agreement with Firestone's demand for "the full restoration to women of ownership over their own bodies."[9] The liberation of women could not be achieved unless women themselves, rather than men and male-dominated institutions (the state, the church, the medical profession), decided whether and when they would bear children.

In the United States in 1970, one key political battle in this area was fought over the right to legal abortion. The Supreme Court's decision in *Roe v. Wade* established that right in 1973, but the issue would remain politically divisive. As the historian Linda Gordon observed in 2002, "No one issue dramatizes the basic cultural/political fissures in the United States at this time more than abortion does."[10] Today it is a central preoccupation of the religious Right, and in many states new restrictions on women's access to it have multiplied. Not only in the United States but in other countries, from Nicaragua to Poland to Pakistan, patriarchal attitudes to women's reproductive rights have not only persisted but have actually hardened during the twenty-first century.

This trend is one example of a bigger challenge confronting feminism today—the rise of new and militant patriarchal movements. These include both modern forms of religious fundamentalism and secular men's rights groups, which often have links to racist and nationalist organizations: white supremacy, male supremacy, and hatred of Muslims and Jews are the main causes of the so-called alt-right. The once-marginal ideologies of these movements have now gained not only influence but real political power. An obvious case in point is the Trump administration, in which (as I write in 2018) a Christian fundamentalist serves as vice president. But the rise of these ideologies isn't just a "first-world problem." Some religious fundamentalist groups in Africa and the Middle East, like Boko Haram and ISIS, have adopted, in the course of their various insurgencies, the ancient patriarchal practice of capturing, raping, and enslaving women and girls. Women's bodily autonomy, both sexual and reproductive, is threatened in both old and new ways, and resisting that threat is therefore high on feminism's current agenda.

But male dominance is not just maintained by the oppressive actions of men and male-dominated institutions: women themselves have often accepted, or been complicit in, their own subordination. Women as well as men support leaders, and vote for governments, that make no secret of their determination to curtail women's rights. Women as well as men are active in social and religious movements that champion traditional (that is, patriarchal) "family values." Why women so often act against what might appear to be their own interests is a question often pondered by feminists, and two kinds of answers have been common.

One answer focuses on the nature of women's relationship with men. Masters may try to win the affection of their servants, slaves, imperial subjects, tenants, or workers (and they may sometimes succeed), but there is no other form of structural inequality that calls for members of the subordinated group to form a lifelong bond of the most intimate kind with a member of the dominant group. Even when women are not dependent on men for protection and subsistence, their love for their husbands, brothers, and sons encourages identification with their interests ("what's good for my family is good for me"). In addition, the patriarchal family in its modern, nuclear form tends to separate women from one another, making it harder for them to develop the kind of collective solidarity that is needed for effective resistance to oppression.

The other answer focuses on the way girls and women are socialized to accept their subordinate position as natural, inevitable, and just. One important agent of this socialization is the family, but others include religion (virtually all the world's major religions have traditionally taught that the subordination of women to men is divinely ordained) and education, or the lack of it. As Gerda Lerner notes, for most of human history almost all women were excluded from advanced learning and so played little part in the creation of knowledge. That exclusion has lessened in recent times, but it will take more than a few decades to undo the effects of thousands of years of male dominance on the way people of both sexes understand the world. The preeminent form of contemporary knowledge, science, continues to be dominated by men: today it could be argued that scientific accounts of male-female differences contribute as much to the maintenance of patriarchy as traditional religious ones. On the other hand, science—like religion before it—can offer women a base from which to challenge male dominance and male-centered knowledge.

It is often argued that both sexes are oppressed by the social arrangements of patriarchal societies. Men may be the dominant sex, but the norms of masculinity subject them to demands that many experience as a burden rather than a privilege. They are expected to suppress their emotions and never show weakness, work long hours to support their families, and risk their lives fighting wars on behalf of their countries. Most feminists would agree that individual men may pay a high price for the collective dominance of their sex. But many would also point out that men benefit from this arrangement in ways women do not. Susan Sontag was critical of what she called "the cliché that when women are liberated men will be liberated too." The idea that patriarchy oppresses everyone equally, she observed, "slides shamelessly over the raw reality of male domination—as if this were an arrangement in fact arranged by nobody, which suits nobody, which works to nobody's advantage."[11] Male dominance persists for the same reason any other system of structural inequality persists: because it does work to somebody's advantage. What feminists hope is that understanding how it works will help us take the actions needed to change it.

2
Rights

Mainstream reference sources agree: feminism is about "women's rights." Oxford Dictionaries defines it as "the advocacy of women's rights on the ground of the equality of the sexes." Wikipedia says that "feminist movements have campaigned and continue to campaign for women's rights." Any search for feminist quotations will also turn up references to women's rights, from "men, their rights and nothing more; women, their rights and nothing less" (the motto of the *Revolution*, a newspaper founded in 1868 by the American suffragists Susan B. Anthony and Elizabeth Cady Stanton) to "women's rights are human rights" (a formula adopted in 1990 by Charlotte Bunch and popularized five years later in a speech by Hillary Clinton).[1]

This mainstream definition is not uncontested. Demands for rights belong to a liberal political tradition, and many feminists would say that their ultimate goal, ending women's oppression, cannot be achieved without more radical social change. From this perspective, defining feminism as a movement for women's rights does not do justice to the breadth of its ambitions. Nevertheless, it is fair to say that the concept of rights has played an important part in feminist politics—both the theory and the practice—throughout the movement's history.

This history begins in the eighteenth century, when philosophical ideas about "the rights of man" were being taken up and acted on by revolutionary political movements. In the famous words of the American Declaration of Independence, written in 1776 by Thomas Jefferson: "We hold these truths to be self-evident, that all men are created equal, that they are endowed by their Creator with certain unalienable rights, that among these are Life, Liberty and the Pursuit of Happiness." The rights being proclaimed here are what theorists call natural rights, which belong to human beings by virtue of their nature (the modern concept of human rights expresses a similar idea). When Jefferson wrote "all men," however, he did not mean all human beings. The men whose rights the declaration asserted were specifically white and male: they did not include slaves or the indigenous people of North America, and they did not include women of any race. Nor were women included in 1789 when revolutionaries in France issued the Declaration of the Rights of Man and of the Citizen. But this omission did not go unopposed. In 1791 the playwright Olympe de Gouges published her own Declaration of the Rights of Woman and of the Female Citizen—one of the offenses for which she was sent to the guillotine two years later. And in England around the same time, another keen observer of events in France, Mary Wollstonecraft, produced what is often seen as the founding philosophical text of the liberal feminist tradition, *A Vindication of the Rights of Woman*.

A Vindication argued that there was no legitimate basis for excluding women from the "rights of man." For thinkers of this time, the defining quality of "man," from which his natural rights derived, was the ability to reason: it was reason that distinguished man from other animals. And when Wollstonecraft used the words "man" and "men" she did mean all human beings. She took issue with the argument that was used to justify withholding rights from women, that they lacked men's capacity for rational thought. Most women, she agreed, had not developed their powers of reason to the same level as most men, but in her view that was a matter of nurture rather than nature, the result of women's inferior education. "Taught from infancy that beauty is woman's sceptre," she wrote, "the mind shapes itself to the body, and roaming round its gilt cage, only seeks to adorn its prison."[2] Women were, nevertheless, rational creatures just as men were, and as such they too were endowed with natural rights.

A Vindication was more philosophical treatise than political manifesto. But in the second half of the nineteenth century, feminists of what we now call the first wave would build on the general argument for women's rights with organized campaigns for specific legal and civil rights. The rights first-wave feminists demanded included women's right to be educated, to earn a living, to enter professions that had previously been closed to them, to own property rather than ceding it to their husbands when they married, to divorce their husbands, and to participate alongside men in political decision-making. This tradition has shaped the popular understanding of feminism as a movement for women's rights—and also the idea that women's rights means equal rights, since the goal of many early campaigns was to secure for women rights that (some) men already had.

Today in most parts of the world this liberal, equal-rights version of feminism has become mainstream common sense. It seems self-evident that women and men should be equal before the law, and only fair that they should have the same rights and opportunities in spheres like education, work, and politics. It is easy to forget how recently this became a matter of consensus. A hundred years ago, no woman in the United States had the right to vote; sex discrimination in employment only became illegal just over fifty years ago; the legal right of a wife to refuse to have sex with her husband was not established in all fifty states until twenty-five years ago. Thinking about what has changed for women during the past century is a salutary reminder of what campaigns for rights have achieved. At the same time, when we think about what hasn't changed, it's clear that the rights approach has limitations.

Some feminists have always rejected equal rights as a "reformist" goal, one that aims to improve women's position in society without radically changing society itself. The American anarchist Emma Goldman, though generally considered a feminist because of her support for the struggles of working women, did not support campaigns for women's suffrage: she saw no virtue in demanding greater privileges within what she described as an inherently unjust political system.[3] In 1969, nearly half a century after the vote had been won in the United States, radical feminists held a protest in which they symbolically handed it back: voting, they maintained, had done nothing to liberate women from patriarchal oppression. Other feminists, however, have defended demands for rights against the criticism that they are insufficiently radical. Some of the strongest arguments on this point have come from Black and indigenous feminists, or those located in the global South, who see feminist critiques of rights as reflecting the perspective of the relatively privileged—white women in Western liberal democracies where basic rights are already well established. In places where the battle is still ongoing (like Saudi Arabia, where women recently won the right to hold driver's licenses but still cannot marry, travel, or sign contracts without the permission of a male guardian), activists do not regard campaigns for rights as irrelevant: they are well aware that cultural norms and attitudes will have to change if women are to be equal citizens in practice, but establishing rights in principle and in law is still a key objective.

One thing just about everyone agrees on is that decades of campaigns, initiatives, and legislation promoting equal rights around the world have not actually delivered equality. Even where the evidence suggests that women's position is improving, their progress appears painfully slow. The much-discussed gender pay gap, for instance, is smaller than it once was, but in 2015 the World Economic Forum predicted that it would not actually close until 2133. Why are goals like equal pay, which command widespread support in theory, so difficult to achieve in practice?

One problem feminists have raised is the tendency for laws to be based on a notion of equality that implicitly requires women to be the same as men in order to be treated equally. For instance, equal pay legislation typically provides a legal remedy for women who can show they are being paid less than men for the same work. What this does not address, however, is the pervasive sex segregation of many labor markets. Large numbers of women earn low wages precisely because they do *not* do the same work as men: they work in traditionally female occupations, or in female-dominated enclaves within a sector that also employs men. Paradoxically, then, the women who are most disadvantaged by the undervaluing of women's work are also the ones who gain least from a formal right to equal pay.

Another issue on which progress has been slow is the underrepresentation of women in political assemblies. In some places this has been addressed by setting quotas to ensure that a certain number of women will be elected. This approach acknowledges the reality that female and male candidates are not competing on the proverbial level playing field: women are disadvantaged by an implicit bias toward men. Measures like quotas are meant to compensate for that bias. But they frequently provoke resistance on the grounds that they are biased themselves: they violate the basic principle of equal rights by not treating men and women identically.

Some rights of particular importance to women cannot easily be justified on the basis that all individuals should be treated identically, because they relate to women's role in reproduction. In the United States, campaigners had to fight a separate battle to establish that discriminating against pregnant women was unlawful under Title VII of the 1964 Civil Rights Act, which had prohibited sex-based discrimination in employment.⁴ Employers maintained that the issue wasn't sex: they weren't refusing to employ women in general, but only women who became pregnant. The women this affected couldn't claim they were being treated less favorably than men in the same position, since there were no men in the same position.

The long and continuing struggle over abortion raises another question about the equal-rights approach: what happens when women's rights are, or are seen to be, in conflict with other rights? In jurisdictions that prohibit abortion, the justification is usually that allowing it would violate the unborn child's right to life. Abortion may be permitted where the mother's own life is threatened, but only her right to life, not her right to bodily autonomy, can take priority over the rights of the fetus. Another argument sometimes used is that mothers should not have rights that fathers are denied. In 2017 it was reported that several US states had either enacted or were considering laws that gave fathers the right to prevent the termination of a pregnancy. This is another case where the "equal treatment without regard to sex" principle is applied without considering the very different positions of men and women. It may take two to conceive a child, but only one can gestate and give birth to it. Giving fathers the power to veto an abortion effectively treats their rights over their unborn children as more important than a woman's rights over her own body.[5]

Abortion is not the only case where conflicting rights may be an issue. The rights of women may also be in tension with general rights such as the right to privacy, to family life, and to the expression of cultural or religious beliefs. This tension reflects the historical origins of the rights framework, which was essentially designed to regulate men's dealings with the government and one another in the public sphere of politics and commerce. It did not reach into the private sphere to regulate men's relationships with other members of their own households—the women, children, servants, and slaves who under the original social contract had no rights of their own. Rather, private life was seen as an area where men should be free from outside interference.

The traces of this idea can still be seen in the text that inaugurated the modern era of human rights, the Universal Declaration of Human Rights (UDHR) adopted by the United Nations General Assembly in 1948. Unlike its eighteenth-century precursors, the declaration explicitly recognized "the equal rights of men and women" in its preamble. But in article 16 it also says that "the family is the natural and fundamental group unit of society and is entitled to protection by society and the State"—an assertion that fails to acknowledge that the family is not an internally homogeneous unit and that the interests of its members may not always coincide. As feminists have been pointing out for decades, a very high proportion of the abuse suffered by women and girls, from forced labor to domestic and sexual violence, is inflicted on them within the family, by other family members. Consequently there is a potential contradiction between the state's duty to protect the family and its duty to protect the equal rights of men and women.

This contradiction is illustrated in many states' responses to the Convention on the Elimination of All Forms of Discrimination against Women (CEDAW), which the UN adopted in 1979. This agreement represented a more concerted effort to address the issue of women's rights: unlike the UDHR, which does not have the force of a treaty, UN conventions impose concrete obligations on member states that ratify them. States are not obliged, however, to ratify every UN convention (the United States chose not to ratify CEDAW), and they also have the option of ratifying a convention while entering reservations—identifying specific obligations that they are not willing to be bound by. In the case of CEDAW the list of reservations was very lengthy, and many of them related to provisions dealing with women's position in the family. Several countries would not recognize a married woman's right to choose her own domicile or her own name, and many insisted that only fathers could pass their nationality on to their children. Malta reserved the right to treat a married woman's income as her husband's for tax purposes, and to pay him, as the head of household, state benefits due to her. Britain (along with Lesotho) wanted to ensure that firstborn sons would continue to inherit the Crown. A number of majority Muslim states (including Bahrain, Egypt, Saudi Arabia, Malaysia, the Maldives, Mauretania, and Morocco) declared that they would not be bound by any provision that conflicted with Islamic law: many expressed specific concerns about the provisions on marriage and divorce, where (in the words of Morocco's reservation) "equality . . . is considered incompatible with the Islamic Shariah, which guarantees to each of the spouses rights and responsibilities within a framework of equilibrium and complementarity."

These reservations illustrate the difficulty of developing an international framework for women's rights. As the legal theorist Catharine MacKinnon has pointed out, gender inequality is a global phenomenon, but attempts to address it globally can be frustrated in two ways. If a form of inequality or oppression is culturally specific, the state(s) concerned can object to the imposition of "alien" cultural norms. This is how so many states were able to ratify a convention whose stated purpose was "the elimination of all forms of discrimination against women" while reserving the right to continue discriminating on such consequential matters as marriage, divorce, inheritance, and nationality. But if a form of gender inequality or oppression is culturally widespread or universal, that may reinforce the argument that it is "only natural" and that the state can do nothing about it.[6]

The observations made by critics like MacKinnon explain why the slogan "women's rights are human rights" is not the tautology it appears to be. It was intended as a reproach to the international human rights movement for its failure to take women's rights, and more especially abuses of their rights, seriously. In 1990 Charlotte Bunch, the American feminist who is widely credited with introducing the slogan (though she has said that she first heard it used by activists in the Philippines), gave a blunt summary of the kind of treatment that excuses like "it's a cultural matter" and "it's only natural" were being used to condone or justify. Women around the world, she noted, "are routinely subject to torture, starvation, terrorism, humiliation, mutilation, and even murder simply because they are female."[7] If these practices targeted some other group, they would surely be seen as obvious human rights violations; but in the case of women that was not how they were seen.

In 1991 activists started a petition calling on the next UN World Conference on Human Rights, which was to be held in 1993 in Vienna, to recognize that "violence against women violates human rights." By the time the petition was presented at the conference, it had been signed by nearly 500,000 people and sponsored by more than 1,000 organizations in 124 countries. Later in the year the UN formally adopted a Declaration on the Elimination of Violence against Women, and the issue has continued to move up the organization's agenda. In 1998 references to gender-based persecution and sexual violence were included in the statute that founded the International Criminal Court; in 2000 the UN adopted a resolution on violence against women in the context of armed conflict. Meanwhile, in 1995, the fourth UN World Conference on Women in Beijing (the event where Hillary Clinton used the expression "women's rights are human rights") produced the Beijing Platform for Action and the associated approach of "gender mainstreaming." Rather than treating women's rights as a separate issue, the UN now integrates a gender perspective into all its work. For any policy or program it plans to adopt, it asks what the impact on women will be (whether positive, negative, or none at all). The same approach is used in monitoring and evaluating policies after they are implemented. The aim is to promote gender equality and, conversely, to avoid perpetuating inequality. In 2010 the Entity for Gender Equality and the Empowerment of Women, more commonly known as UN Women, was established to support both UN policymakers and the efforts of member states to implement international standards.[8]

I have focused on the UN because its policies and standards are so widely influential, not only for the governments of member states but also for nongovernmental organizations around the world. The developments in its approach to women's rights since 1990 have had a significant impact, especially in making violence against women a higher priority. But the question of how women's rights are defined and understood remains a complex and challenging one, especially for a movement that aspires to be global, intersectional, and inclusive. The documents I have mentioned or quoted in this chapter typically treat women as an undifferentiated category, defined by the simple contrast with men. But in reality, of course, women are not undifferentiated: their situations and needs are shaped by differences of age, class, race, ethnicity, sexuality, religious belief or nonbelief, marital status, maternal status, rural versus urban location, and location in the global South versus the North. Just as there may be conflicts between the rights of women and those of men or of children, so there may also be conflicts between different groups of women. To illustrate this, let us briefly consider some cases where women and feminists have been divided on the issue of rights.

The first case takes us back to the campaign for legal abortion in the United States. As Angela Davis pointed out in *Women, Race and Class*, this was a campaign dominated by white women, and regarded with some suspicion by many Black women and women of color.[9] That was not because those women did not need or want the right to terminate a pregnancy legally. Davis cites statistics showing that in the state of New York, before abortion was decriminalized, a large majority of the women who died following illegal abortions were Black or Puerto Rican. But the campaign for abortion rights failed to take on board what, for nonwhite and poor women, was an equally pressing concern: the "sterilization abuse" that denied their right to choose to have children. Black, Latina, and Native American women, along with the most impoverished white women, were being targeted by programs that bribed or coerced them into undergoing sterilization (for instance, by offering the procedure free of charge when birth control was not free, or by threatening to withdraw welfare benefits unless they agreed to be sterilized); there were also cases where women and teenage girls were sterilized without their consent.

As Davis explains, these programs continued an older tradition of eugenicist efforts to "improve" the quality of the population and alleviate social problems like poverty, unemployment, and crime by preventing the "unfit" from reproducing. In the context of the United States, ideas about fitness were strongly influenced by racist and white supremacist ideologies. White feminist advocates of birth control and abortion rights did not always avoid reproducing these beliefs, and in some cases they clearly shared them.[10] Even when they did not, their own experiences (which included being refused when they requested sterilization) made them reluctant to address other women's concerns about sterilization abuse. On this point, it seemed, there was a conflict between the rights of the most and the least privileged women. But in Davis's intersectional analysis, the experiences of both groups can be understood as different manifestations of the same underlying problem, the way women's reproductive capacities are regulated in the interests of powerful white men. Those interests dictate that women who belong to an "inferior" racial group should be denied the right to reproduce, while women who belong to the dominant group are effectively forced to reproduce. In neither case are women's own wishes respected. For Davis it follows that an effective movement for reproductive rights must begin from the principle that all women have the right to control their own fertility, whether it is a matter of choosing to have children or of choosing not to have them. This is neither a contradiction nor a token gesture of inclusiveness: without it, campaigns for reproductive rights will not only condone racism, they will be conceptually incoherent.

The view of reproductive rights that Davis elaborated is

now widely accepted among feminists. But recently a new conflict has emerged on another issue relating to reproduction: commercial surrogacy, an arrangement under which a person or couple commissions and pays a woman to gestate and give birth to a child for them. This has become a transnational form of commerce, both for reasons of cost (it follows the same logic that has led to offshoring in other industries) and legality (the practice is prohibited in some countries, prompting clients who cannot legally purchase the service at home to look for providers overseas). In various parts of Asia, for instance, there are clinics that recruit women to act as surrogates, oversee the necessary medical procedures, and in some cases run hostels where women can be monitored during pregnancy.

This trade has prompted debate about the rights of both the surrogates and the clients.[11] Although feminists now generally accept a definition of reproductive rights that encompasses women's right to have children as well as their right not to, opponents of commercial surrogacy maintain that there is no right to exploit another woman for that purpose. Where the surrogates are women from poor communities in the global South, campaigners argue that the transaction is unavoidably exploitative and puts the women involved at risk of abuse (for instance, they might be coerced into surrogacy by families desperate for money or be subjected to treatments whose long-term effects they are not fully informed of). Other feminists, however, see these arguments as denying women agency and choice. If feminists believe in women's right to bodily autonomy, that surely means poor women in South and Southeast Asia have a right to sell their services as gestational surrogates (similar arguments are made about the sale of sexual services, a question I will explore in chapter 5). For feminists who take this view, there is no conflict between the rights of the client and those of the surrogate, and outlawing surrogacy would unfairly restrict the rights of both.

This debate raises a more general question that relates to many other discussions of rights. We often talk about rights, not to mention agency and choice, as if they were exercised in a vacuum, when in reality what we can or cannot do depends on the conditions in which we operate. In the surrogacy case, for instance, we are dealing with choices that no one could have made before the advent of new reproductive technologies. Women's choices are also shaped by the extreme economic inequality that makes this business model viable—affordable for overseas clients, economically worthwhile for local surrogates, and profitable for the clinics. If women in places like rural Gujarat had more and better economic options, how many would choose to be gestational surrogates for wealthy foreigners? In the nineteenth century it could have been said that millions of women in the West chose to enter domestic service—but when other options became available during and after World War I, the supply of live-in servants diminished rapidly.

Another question on which feminists are divided concerns the cultural and religious rights of minority women. In Europe there is particular controversy about the public wearing of religious symbols, especially the *niqab* or face veil worn by some Muslim women, which is now prohibited in France and Belgium; there has also been some debate about the role played by religious courts in arbitrating marital and family disputes. The context in which these matters are discussed is one of rising anti-Muslim racism. Many feminists, along with leftists and liberals more generally, understand measures like the banning of the *niqab* as a form of discrimination motivated primarily by racism, and are outraged when the authorities responsible claim to be motivated by concerns about the rights of Muslim women.[12] In addition to denouncing these claims as cynical, some feminists have condemned them for presenting Muslim women as helpless victims in need of rescue by Western liberals. Many Muslim women have objected both to the assumption that they have not made their own choices and to the idea that non-Muslim feminists should debate what is oppressive to Muslim women rather than taking their cue from what those women say themselves.

Undoubtedly it is important to listen to what Muslim women say. But political arguments about rights are rarely settled by calls to listen to what women from a particular group say, because listening to them soon reveals that they are not all saying the same thing. The fact that women share an identity does not guarantee they will share the same political analysis. There are feminists who support religious rights for women in Muslim and other minority communities; there are also feminists from the same communities who take the opposing view.

An example of the second type is Southall Black Sisters (SBS), a British feminist group with a long record of campaigning for the rights of Black and South Asian women. In recent years the group has become increasingly concerned about the role played by religious courts in dealing with certain kinds of legal disputes in minority communities (in particular, those relating to "family matters" like marriage, divorce, custody, inheritance, and domestic violence). So long as the parties to a dispute have agreed to use these courts, their decisions are now recognized by the state. SBS opposes this use of religious courts, maintaining that there should be "one law for all." Its campaign on this issue is framed as a defense of minority women's right to equal citizenship as well as equal treatment. Part of the problem is that religious courts often do not treat women equally, as was noted in a 2016 campaign statement signed by three hundred women: "We know from personal experiences that many religious bodies . . . are presided over by hardline or fundamentalist clerics who abuse their positions of power by shaming and slandering those of us who reject aspects of our religions and cultures that we find oppressive. We pay a huge price for not submitting to domestic violence, rape, polygamy and child abuse."[13] But SBS also regards the acceptance of religious courts alongside secular ones as problematic in its own right because it creates an invidious distinction between minority women and the majority. It allows minority women's status as members of a particular community or religious faith to take precedence over their status as citizens of the nation, and leaves their rights to be adjudicated by a parallel justice system whose workings are neither transparent nor democratically accountable.

Other feminists, however, have made the opposite argument—that the insistence on one law for all effectively denies some minority women the same access to justice as other citizens. Women with certain beliefs may have needs that they cannot satisfy through a secular court, such as a religiously valid divorce that leaves them free to remarry.[14] Once again, the underlying question here is about the balance between sameness and difference: does equality require that everyone be treated the same, or can some kinds of equality only be achieved by *not* treating everyone identically?

Rights and equality are familiar, mainstream concepts, but they are not always as simple as they appear. And while rights do have an important place in feminism, both historically and in the present, they are only one part of the bigger picture. Without other kinds of change—social, cultural, and economic—the rights women possess on paper may do little in practice to improve their lives.

3
Work

What would you expect to find in a chapter about feminist perspectives on work? I'm guessing that your answer might include a discussion of the gender pay gap, the underrepresentation of women in certain employment sectors, the glass ceiling, and the problem of what's often called the work-life balance. These subjects are all featured prominently in media coverage of "women's issues": the attention they receive both reflects and reinforces the popular belief that getting women into the workplace—and especially into high-status careers—is one of the main goals, if not *the* main goal, of feminism. That assumption has prompted conservatives to complain that feminism devalues women's traditional role in the home, while radicals complain that it focuses too narrowly on the first-world problems of elite professional women. Both criticisms, however, could be said to attack a straw feminism. Feminist ideas about work are more varied and more complicated than the popular stereotype acknowledges.

Popular discussions of women and work often equate "work" specifically with *paid* work—labor that is exchanged for money, in the form of wages, fees, or a salary. Our everyday conversations make the same equation. For instance, people ask new mothers whether they plan to go "back to work," as if looking after a baby were not work. One of the defining features of a feminist perspective is the recognition that caring for your family is also work: the difference is that you don't get paid for it. And that is a feminist issue, because most unpaid care work for the family is done by women. That fact is often invoked as a commonsense explanation for things like the gender pay gap ("women earn less than men because they have family responsibilities"). But for feminists it isn't good enough to treat women's family responsibilities as self-evident: we need to explain why only women are expected to perform this balancing act, and why it is seen as a problem for individual women to solve rather than an issue for society as a whole.

Another problem with the familiar list of "women and work" issues is that many of them are easily seen as the concerns of a small and highly privileged minority. Most women around the world don't have the luxury of worrying about career choices and glass ceilings: they work to pay the rent and put food on the table. Elite professional women are not just in a different situation from less privileged women, their high-powered careers may depend on those women's labor as cleaners, housekeepers, nannies, and babysitters.[1] These jobs are done predominantly by working-class women, women of color, and migrant women from poorer parts of the world, whose situation, working and sometimes also living in their employer's home, can leave them vulnerable to exploitation and abuse. Charities and nongovernmental organizations have documented many cases where the conditions of work amount to slavery, with workers forbidden to leave the house, forced to work without wages, deprived of their passports, and subjected to physical and sexual violence.[2]

Feminism does have to consider the situation of all women, not just some; it must be able to deal with differences and inequalities between women, and with the exploitation of some by others. But as I noted in the introduction, one of feminism's core beliefs is that women are oppressed *as women*. So, a feminist analysis must also ask how relationships among women (including unequal or exploitative ones) are affected by the fact that those involved are women rather than men.

For instance, we might ask why the exploitation of poor women's domestic labor is so often presented as the exclusive responsibility of wealthier women. From a feminist perspective there's another party to this transaction, even if he remains discreetly in the background: the man of the household. This particular form of exploitation is shaped by the assumption that a wife is responsible for taking care of the house and the children; if she doesn't want to provide those services herself, it's her responsibility to find a substitute. Her husband benefits from this arrangement as much as she does: without it he would either have to share the work or accept a lower standard of service. But he is not seen as the exploiter, because he hasn't chosen to pay someone else to do "his" job.

It might be argued (and often has been) that the wife in a household rich enough to pay for domestic help is making a choice: she isn't going out to work because she has to, but because she wants to. Many poorer women would envy her freedom to stay at home. But this argument overlooks another point. Whatever her class or lifestyle, a woman who has no paid job will in most cases be financially dependent on her husband's earnings. That dependence is a form of inequality which not only disadvantages her in their relationship (without an income of her own she will find it hard to escape if he abuses her, for instance), it also contributes to the economic disadvantage women collectively suffer. The idea that women can depend on the income of a male breadwinner has persistently been used to justify paying all women lower wages, and that exacerbates the poverty of many households that do, in fact, depend on women's earnings. These are all reasons why feminists since the nineteenth century have seen access to paid work as an important political demand. And it isn't just important for the most privileged Western women.

In 1990 the economist Amartya Sen wrote an article entitled "More Than 100 Million Women Are Missing."[3] He based this claim on an analysis of population statistics showing that in certain parts of the world, like North Africa and much of Asia, men are significantly more numerous than women. In China in the 1980s the ratio was 94 women for every 100 men. In the Indian state of Punjab it was 86 women to 100 men. These figures are striking, Sen explains, because they reverse the expected pattern. More boys than girls are born (the normal ratio is about 105 to 100), but because infant mortality is higher among boys, while at the other end of the age spectrum life expectancy is greater for women, the norm—other things being equal—is for the overall population to contain a slightly higher percentage of women. Exceptions arise when other things are not equal: when girls and women are not valued, or treated, equally, and the result is disproportionately high rates of female mortality. Girls and women die because they are not given enough to eat or because they do not receive the medical care they need. In some cases, infant girls are deliberately neglected or even killed. And today we know that many girls are never born, because families use sex-selective abortion to avoid having daughters.

Sen does not think this is just a case of females losing out to males where economic resources are scarce. He notes that men do not outnumber women in most of sub-Saharan Africa, a region with some of the world's poorest countries; in India too, the imbalance is greater in Punjab, a relatively wealthy state, than in Kerala, a much poorer one. The real issue, he argues, is how resources are distributed within households. And this, he believes, can be related to the question of women's work: in particular, whether women engage in productive labor that makes a tangible contribution to the household economy. His analysis suggests that women are valued more, and treated better, when they are "gainfully employed," earning money outside the household.

Women who are not "gainfully employed" are nevertheless, as Sen recognizes, working. Typically, they are spending many hours each day on activities like cooking, cleaning, washing and mending clothes, and caring for children, the old, and the sick. In some of the societies he discusses they may also be undertaking such time-consuming tasks as collecting water and gathering firewood. But this work is, as he puts it, "unpaid and unhonored." Its real economic value goes unrecognized because its products are largely intangible. Housework is classed as "reproductive" rather than productive work: it enables other members of the household to engage in productive labor by freeing them from tasks like food preparation that they would otherwise have to do for themselves. And this is not just an issue for women in North Africa or Punjab. Reproductive work has to be done in every society, and in every society that has consequences for women.

In 2014, the Organisation for Economic Co-operation and Development (OECD) reported that "around the world, women spend two to ten times more time on unpaid care work than men."[4] As this wording implies, differences exist between regions and countries (as well as between social classes—typically, the poorer the household, the greater the gap). In India, where the disparity between men and women is particularly large, the average time spent on unpaid care work is six hours a day for women compared with thirty-six minutes for men. But even where the disparity is much smaller, women still do around twice as much unpaid work as men. In North America, for instance, the male mean is just over two hours and the female mean is just under four. This unequal division of domestic labor affects women's position in the paid labor market. Where housework is very time consuming, women cannot engage in paid work at all; where it is slightly less time consuming they may be limited to part-time, casual, and low-paid jobs. Domestic responsibilities may also make it impossible for women and girls to take up the education and training opportunities that would improve their employment prospects and their earning abilities.

The OECD sees this problem as a serious one for developing countries since it means they cannot make full use of women's labor power in their drive to increase economic growth. The report recommends various measures governments can take to address the situation: they can invest in infrastructure to reduce the time housework takes (if more households in Ghana had electricity, fewer women would have to spend time collecting firewood), expand public services like nurseries and daycare centers for the elderly (the report mentions a project in Kenya where mobile crèches were provided for the children of women working on a construction site), introduce family-friendly policies (like flexible hours and parental leave), and try to tackle "entrenched social norms and gender stereotypes" in an effort to "'de-feminise' care-giving" and so encourage men to do more of it.[5]

It's notable that only the last of these recommendations deals directly with the inequality between the sexes. The others are designed to reduce the burden on women without transferring any of it to men. The difficulty of redistributing unpaid work within households is suggested by the OECD's own statistics. In rich countries, particularly the welfare states of western Europe, families already have access to time-saving technology, childcare facilities, and flexible working hours, but it's still women who do more unpaid care work. Why is this division of labor so persistent? How should we analyze it, and what could or should be done about it? Like all the other questions discussed in this book, these questions have prompted debate and disagreement among feminists. The rest of this chapter will explore some of the competing analyses, theories, and proposals they have put forward. I'll begin, though, by considering how we got to where we are now.

Most human societies appear to have had some kind of sexual division of labor, with some tasks assigned to women and others to men. In small-scale traditional societies this arrangement has often been described as egalitarian: the two sexes are economically interdependent, in that each needs the products of the other's labor. There do not seem to be many forms of work that are universally reserved for men or women: the same task—for instance, cultivating corn—may be a man's job in one group and a woman's job in another.

In larger and more complex pre-industrial societies, like those of medieval and early modern Europe, historians have pointed to elements of both hierarchy and reciprocity in the organization of men's and women's work. Before the Industrial Revolution, most production was based in the household, and much of it was for use rather than for sale. This mode of production required the labor of both sexes: for instance, men might tend the cattle, but women butchered and preserved meat, churned butter, and made fat into candles. A woman married to an artisan or merchant often learned her husband's trade and assisted with his work; sometimes she acted as her husband's agent or took over the business after her husband died. This arrangement cannot be called gender egalitarian, because marriage was not a relationship of equals. In England (and later its colonies), married women were subject to coverture, a legal provision stipulating that a wife had no existence independent of her husband: her property, earnings, and services all belonged to him. Wives who worked alongside their husbands were not equal partners. But the fact that their contribution was needed gave them some leverage: the dependence was mutual rather than all one way.

The Industrial Revolution changed this. Most production gradually moved out of the household and into the factories and mills where men, women, and children worked for wages. Domestic labor then became a primarily reproductive rather than productive activity. Instead of producing the things the household used, like food, beer, clothing, and candles, the housewife performed the domestic services, like cooking, cleaning, and laundry, that enabled members of the household to keep going out to work. The wages they earned could then be used to buy what would once have been produced at home. Providing domestic services did not so much become as remain a female responsibility (the tasks involved were ones women had done in the past); what changed was the conditions in which this work was done. In the new industrial economy, home and the workplace became distinct domains. A woman who worked for wages was now obliged to carry out domestic tasks like cooking and cleaning when she was not "at work"; in effect she was required to work a second shift.

Many women did enter the industrial workforce, but their wages were always lower than men's, and this led to conflict. Men argued that they should not have to compete with women, who were cheaper to employ, or settle for lower wages themselves. The idea began to gain ground that men should be paid enough to support a family, while women should prioritize their domestic responsibilities, ideally working outside the home only to supplement the wages of the family breadwinner. This "male breadwinner with dependent housewife" arrangement is what people today usually mean when they talk about the "traditional" family or women's "traditional" role—but historically speaking it is not really traditional at all. Nor was it ever a universal norm in practice. However, it has been argued that it came to be seen as the ideal, not only because it suited men, but also because it served the interests of capitalism. Women whose main occupation was understood to be in the home formed a cheap and convenient reserve army of labor—a Marxist term for a group of un- or underemployed people who can be pulled into the workforce when they are needed (when the economy is booming, for instance, or in wartime, to replace men who are serving in the armed forces) and then pushed out again when recession, or peace, makes them superfluous. In the case of women, this could be justified by saying that they already had a job at home, and that their paid jobs were needed by men with families to support.

But there's a reason why I've been using the past tense. The current neoliberal and globalized form of capitalism offers other options for reducing costs and maximizing profits: for instance, recruiting foreign workers who are willing to accept lower wages, or putting workers on contracts that require them to be available for work yet do not guarantee them any. Companies can also move some of their operations to parts of the world where costs are lower, or they can invest in technology, which lessens their dependence on human labor. The workers whose position has been most dramatically affected by these practices are not women but first-world working-class men: the industrial manufacturing jobs they once held have moved overseas or been automated, while most newly created jobs are less secure, lower-paid ones in the female-dominated service sector.

These changes have made the old model of a working man supporting his wife and children on a single "family wage" increasingly remote from most people's real-life experience; but it remains powerful in the cultural imagination. The recent surge of right-wing populism in the United States and many parts of Europe has been fueled not only by racism and xenophobia, but also by nostalgia for the golden age of the male breadwinner. Part of Donald Trump's appeal to American voters (especially less-educated white men) rested on his promise to bring back the well-paid, secure jobs that once gave men authority in their homes and status in their communities. The same nostalgia is clearly visible in a letter written to a Utah newspaper in 2017. The writer, a local Republican, called on state legislators to reject a bill mandating equal pay for men and women on the grounds that men "need to make enough to support their families and allow the Mother to remain in the home to raise and nurture the children."[6] This argument presupposes not only that it is desirable for women to be dependent on a male breadwinner, but also that all women have that option. In reality, many do not: whether because they are single (unmarried, divorced, widowed) or because the men they live with are unemployed, they are obliged to be breadwinners themselves. This was also true in the so-called golden age—and indeed for hundreds of years before it. There have always been households that depended on women's earnings. Paying women less than men condemns many of those households to poverty. That is one reason (the other being the basic principle of fairness) why feminists have long supported laws like the one the Utah writer opposes.

But the gender pay gap is not just a consequence of employers' paying women less than men for doing the same job, as we can see from the fact that it persists in places where equal pay laws have been in force for many years. Sex segregation exists in many areas of the labor market: women and men do different jobs, and jobs done by women are undervalued precisely because they are done by women.[7] Some of those jobs are seen as extensions of the unpaid work women do at home, and as such are assumed to require no skill. When I worked in a hospital laundry in the mid-1970s, the men, whose job was loading and unloading washing machines, were paid nearly 50 percent more than women who ironed surgical gowns and nurses' uniforms. (If you don't think ironing demands more skill than loading a washing machine, you clearly haven't done much laundry.)

Another factor that contributes to the pay gap is that many women take time out from paid work, or work part-time, while caring for their young children. Consequently they earn less than their continuously employed and full-time counterparts, take longer to climb whatever career ladder may exist, and end up with smaller pensions. This way of balancing the competing demands of "work and family" (or put another way, paid and unpaid work) is often talked about as a choice individual women make. But the language of choice glosses over the ways in which women's choices are constrained by structural factors they have no control over. Even before they have children, many women will be earning less than their male partners, making it rational in economic terms for the mother to become the primary or full-time parent. Then there are the cultural factors referred to by the OECD as "entrenched social norms and gender stereotypes."[8] There is a strong social expectation that the primary caregiver for children will be their mother: many men either do not want to take that role or worry about how employers will perceive them if they do. Last but not least, there is the way most paid work is organized, which presupposes that full-time workers can delegate unpaid care work to someone else. A simple illustration is the fact that the standard working day is longer than the standard school day or the standard opening hours of a doctor's office. For feminists it is not enough to say that individual women should have choices. We need to ask why things are arranged in a way that obliges women to make certain choices, and whether we could or should make different arrangements. Many feminist discussions of work have revolved around these questions, but different feminists have approached them in different ways.

Socialist and Marxist feminists have been particularly interested in understanding the place of women's work in the larger economic and social structure. Who benefits from the current arrangements? Their answer is that women's work—both paid and unpaid—does not just benefit their families, but also capitalism and the state. Capitalists get a reserve army of cheap labor and the services of workers who have been fed and otherwise cared for at no cost to their employer. The state saves on public services, because women do so much caregiving either for nothing or in exchange for very minimal welfare benefits. This Marxist analysis emphasizes the economic value of the domestic services women provide, and one proposal that has come out of it is that the state should compensate women by paying them wages for housework.[9] This might in theory solve two of the problems mentioned earlier: the lack of security and autonomy that results from the housewife's financial dependence on her husband, and the burden of working an unpaid second shift. But there are other problems it would not solve: it leaves the sexual division of labor unchallenged (if women get paid to do housework, men have even less incentive to share it), and it does not address the argument that doing domestic labor in your own home is inherently so isolating and unrewarding that it should not be anyone's full-time occupation.

Other feminists have argued that a more enlightened goal would be to free women from household drudgery. Angela Davis suggested that this could be achieved by shifting from the pre-industrial mode housework was stuck in (every woman doing the same repetitive tasks in and for her own household) to a more industrial one, in which workers equipped with high-tech cleaning machines would go from home to home performing the same work in a fraction of the time.[10] For Shulamith Firestone the solution was not to industrialize but to collectivize housework and childcare by creating alternatives to the nuclear family, an institution she saw as central to the oppression of both women and children. She acknowledged that previous experiments along these lines, such as the early Soviet communes, had not always been popular with women, but she rejected the argument that the family was the only institution that could meet people's needs for intimacy and care. In her view the problem with the Soviet experiment was that it had not given proper consideration to those needs; rather, it had simply drafted women into a system of production designed for men.

The same criticism could be made of contemporary capitalist societies. They are keen to integrate women into the male world of productive work, where they will help to generate economic growth, but efforts to draft men into the female world of caregiving often do not go much beyond pious exhortations like the OECD's call to tackle entrenched social norms and gender stereotypes. The basic problem with this approach is hinted at in something else the OECD says—that caregiving needs to be "de-feminized" to encourage men's participation. Whereas women can expect to gain status by doing what was traditionally defined as men's work, men perceive care work as something that will lower both their status and their earnings. Katrine Marçal notes that in Sweden, the care assistant who comforts a dying elderly woman receives an hourly wage of sixty-nine kronor (about eight dollars)—significantly less than, say, a real estate agent or a security guard would earn.[11] The OECD talks about defeminizing caregiving, but if we want real equality between the sexes, we will also need to demasculinize the values and assumptions of the workplace so that it no longer seems natural to pay someone who sells or guards property more than someone who cares for the old, the sick, and the dying.

More generally, we need to stop basing every aspect of the way work is organized on the assumption that the prototypical worker is a man. Even so-called family-friendly policies are usually conceived as concessions to women's "special needs." In 2017, for instance, some researchers in Australia suggested that women's working hours should be cut to a maximum of thirty-four per week (compared with a male maximum of forty-seven) to compensate for the extra time women spent on domestic duties.[12] If this measure were adopted, its negative consequences—employers trying to avoid hiring women, and men refusing to share the domestic duties ("it's your job, you get time off for it")—would likely outweigh the benefits. A more radical approach would be to shorten the working week for everyone, on the assumption that the prototypical worker, regardless of sex, has domestic and caregiving responsibilities.

Women's relationship to work is shaped not only by institutional and societal factors (such as the laws and policies of the state, the workings of capitalism, and the demands of employers) but also by more personal ones. Work-related issues (like time and money and housework and childcare) cause conflict between men and women, and these exemplify the feminist principle that the personal is political. At bottom, what's at issue is power: who has the obligation to do what for whom, and who has authority over whom.

When I was growing up, it was common for people to ask married women if their husbands "let" them go out to work or "minded" if they had a job. (Then as now, questions based on the opposite premise—"do you mind your husband having a job?" or "do you let your husband do housework?"—would have been absurd.) These questions presupposed that women were subject to the authority of their husbands, and that men might see a wife's paid employment as a threat to their authority. Today there is less opposition to women having jobs (in many households their income is essential), but research suggests it remains quite common for men to resent it if their female partners earn more than they do. Some studies suggest that men whose female partners earn more than they do spend even less time on domestic chores, and one study has found men in this position are more likely to cheat on their partners.[13] This can't be explained in purely economic terms: it has more to do with ideas about masculinity and the proper relationship between the sexes.

I began this chapter by referring to one popular view of feminism as a kind of propaganda campaign urging women to discover the joys of paid work while devaluing their traditional domestic role. The reality is more complicated. While feminists hold a range of views, they all begin from an understanding that the issue is not whether to work or stay at home. For most women, home *is* a place of work. Rather, the question is how to negotiate the demands of work, both paid and unpaid, in a world that is organized around men's needs rather than women's.

4
Femininity

In her introduction to *The Second Sex*, Simone de Beauvoir remarked on a paradox: "Everyone agrees there are females in the human species; today, as in the past, they make up about half of humanity. And yet we are told that 'femininity is in jeopardy'; we are urged, 'Be women, stay women, become women.' So not every female human being is necessarily a woman; she must take part in this mysterious and endangered reality known as femininity."[1] In the 1940s, when Beauvoir was writing, both popular and much expert wisdom was what we would now call essentialist. It held that the "essence" of Woman—her universal and unchanging nature—was determined by her biological and reproductive functions. Femininity, it followed, was just the natural expression of femaleness. Beauvoir argued that this was, at the very least, an oversimplification. The word "woman" denotes not just a biological category but, more importantly, a social one, and to be recognized as a member of the social category, it is not sufficient to have been born female. It is also necessary to have acquired the modes of behavior deemed appropriate for women in a particular time and place. Hence Beauvoir's famous statement that "one is not born, but rather becomes, a woman."[2] This insight was taken up by the English-speaking feminists of the post-1968 second wave, who made a theoretical distinction between *sex*, meaning biological maleness and femaleness, and *gender*, meaning culturally defined (or socially constructed, to use the formulation that has since become more common) masculinity and femininity.

One important piece of evidence that femininity is socially constructed is that what counts as feminine is not universal and unchanging: it can vary significantly across cultures and over time. Another influential thinker of the mid-twentieth century, the American anthropologist Margaret Mead, drew attention to striking differences in the social roles and personality traits that were considered normal and desirable for men and women in different societies. In *Sex and Temperament*, a study of three traditional societies in Papua New Guinea that was first published in 1935, Mead compared the Tchambuli people, a group in which women took charge and men were seen as the less capable, more passive, and more emotional sex, with two other groups, the Arapesh and the Mundugumor, where the same qualities were valued in both sexes, but they were different qualities in each case. Among the Arapesh both sexes were peaceable, whereas among the Mundugumor they were both aggressive. Mead concluded that human nature was extremely plastic, and that the way it developed in individuals owed more to the influence of culture than to the dictates of biology.[3]

To say this is not to deny that some experiences that are common to many women in all times and places *are* shaped by their biology (for instance, almost all women experience menstruation, and the majority also experience pregnancy and childbirth). But among humans, even the most basic and universal experiences (such as eating or dying, to take two examples that are not sex specific) are always embedded in culture. How women actually experience biological processes like menstruation or pregnancy will be influenced not only by the nature of the processes themselves but also by the way those processes are understood and dealt with in the society the women belong to.

A great deal of what has to be learned in the process of becoming a woman has no obvious connection to biological femaleness at all. No biological sex difference can explain, for instance, why my brother's school shirts buttoned in the opposite direction from mine, or why our parents scolded me, but not him, for whistling or for sitting with my legs apart. These behaviors were not unfemale (I, a female person, was perfectly capable of engaging in them); rather, they were unfeminine—or as my parents more often said, "unladylike," meaning at odds with a particular norm of upper-class femininity. The very fact that we can describe a woman's behavior or appearance as unfeminine without being accused of talking self-contradictory nonsense is another piece of evidence that femininity is different from femaleness. As Susan Brownmiller observes, femininity "always demands more. It must constantly reassure its audience by a willing demonstration of difference, even when one does not exist in nature, or it must seize and embrace a natural variation and compose a rhapsodic symphony upon the notes."[4] Femininity is not just a cultural construct but a cultural imposition—a set of expectations, prescriptions, and prohibitions enforced through a system of rewards and punishments. These attempts at enforcement are not, of course, guaranteed to work: many women, past and present, have rejected conventional femininity, and few if any of us embody our culture's idealized notions of the feminine completely and consistently. But while we may be able to choose how far we will conform to expectations, the consequences are not a matter of individual choice. As a child I could choose to whistle, but I couldn't prevent the people around me from understanding my behavior as "unladylike" and judging it accordingly (which usually meant negatively).

What about masculinity? Isn't that also a cultural construct, something male-born people have to learn the rules for—like "boys don't cry" or "real men don't show their feelings"? And don't men also get rewarded or punished for conforming to or deviating from the masculine norm? In short, isn't the binary gender system limiting and oppressive for everyone? The short answer is yes: if femininity is socially constructed, then the same must be true of masculinity. These are relational terms, defined by contrast with each other. Beauvoir argued, however, that their relationship is not symmetrical: the masculine is both the positive and the neutral term (she points out that the word *homme*, like its English equivalent, "man," can designate either a male human or the human species in general), whereas the feminine represents only the negative. Gender, from this perspective, is not just a system of social categorization based on a contrast between two equal-but-opposite terms: it is a hierarchy in which the masculine outranks the feminine. While some gender distinctions may be arbitrary and trivial, others can be linked more directly to the social system in which men exercise power while women play a secondary, supporting role. Masculinity is active, assertive, rational, strong, and courageous; femininity is passive, submissive, emotional, weak, and in need of protection. The qualities women are encouraged to cultivate are the ones used to justify their inferior social status.

It is undoubtedly true that many individual men and boys experience the demands of masculinity as oppressive, and for some they are deeply damaging. Men who are judged insufficiently masculine can face severe sanctions; at the extreme, the penalty may be death. But while feminists acknowledge that the binary gender system has negative consequences for both sexes, at a structural level it is also part of the apparatus that maintains inequality between men and women. Feminists also want to change the system, though as usual they do not agree on what to do about it. Some are gender "abolitionists," advocating a world in which, to quote Shulamith Firestone, "genital differences between human beings would no longer matter culturally,"[5] while others would like individuals to be free to choose from a more diverse array of gender identities (I return to this debate in chapter 7). There are also many feminists who are less interested in overthrowing the system and more concerned to challenge the narrowness and rigidity of its current norms.

In the rest of this chapter I will look more closely at two sets of questions about femininity that have featured prominently in both feminist theoretical analysis and feminist political activism since the 1960s. One set of questions concerns something almost all feminists have seen as oppressive: the impact on girls and women of normative expectations about their bodily appearance. The other, which I will begin with, concerns the way the norms of femininity (and masculinity) are acquired during the formative years of childhood.

Since Beauvoir expounded it in 1949, the antiessentialist argument that "one is not born a woman" has faced repeated challenges, and one of the great battlegrounds in this debate is the question of child development. Those who argue that male-female differences are products of nature rather than nurture very often appeal to evidence showing that these differences emerge very early in life, before children become aware of social norms and expectations. They also point to the apparent failure of nonsexist child-rearing practices to eliminate the differences. However they are raised, it seems, girls and boys just "naturally" prefer to do, wear, and play with different things.

This "only natural" argument was challenged during the feminist second wave and fell briefly out of fashion, but in recent decades it has become popular again, influentially championed by the evolutionary psychologists whose account of human nature I mentioned in chapter 2. Evolutionary psychologists explain differences between the sexes with reference to the purposes they would hypothetically have served among our earliest human ancestors, and it sometimes seems there is nothing that cannot be fitted into this narrative. In 2007 some researchers even suggested that the attraction of the color pink for young girls in the twenty-first century might be a product of nature rather than culture, reflecting the importance of pink (the color of many edible berries) for the female gatherers of human prehistory. Conversely, boys' preference for blue might go back to the time when prehistoric hunters spent hours scanning the sky. But historians pointed out a flaw in this story: there is nothing ancient about the association of pink with girls and blue with boys. On the contrary, as recently as the early twentieth century pink was considered a masculine color (a milder version of red, and as such particularly suitable for young boys), while blue was regarded as more feminine.[6]

Why are we so receptive to the kinds of stories evolutionary psychology tells? In part, perhaps, because gender distinctions often do present themselves to us in everyday life as fixed and intractable. If you are a parent whose daughter insists, despite all your objections, that everything she owns must be pink, it is easy to feel that her intransigence must be produced by something more profound than a mere cultural norm. We tend to think of nature or biology as deep and culture as shallow and superficial. But this is a mistake: culture is also deep. Many feminists over the years have sought to document the processes through which gendered ways of seeing, thinking, and acting are imposed on and ingrained in children from the moment of their birth.

Some of this documentation comes from controlled scientific studies measuring, for instance, how long mothers spend verbally interacting with young children (typically this research has found they interact more with girls than with boys), or how a child's sex affects adults' assessments of their physical abilities (we tend to overestimate what boys can manage while underestimating what girls of the same age can do). This body of research provides evidence that male and female children really are treated differently from the very beginning, in ways that do have the potential to affect their subsequent development. It also offers evidence of the phenomenon the psychologist Cordelia Fine calls "parenting with a half-changed mind."[7] Even adults who consciously oppose gender stereotyping, and who genuinely believe they are treating their sons and their daughters identically, still seem to be influenced at a subconscious level by stereotypes, such as girls being verbally expressive and boys being physically adventurous.

Another psychologist, Bronwyn Davies, studied preschool children's own attempts to make sense of the differences between girls and boys. She observed that they were receiving mixed messages from adults: liberal parents and teachers discouraged "extreme" expressions of masculinity and femininity—they didn't want ultra-aggressive, emotionally insensitive boys or girls who were passive shrinking violets in frilly dresses—but at the same time they demanded that the children be intelligible as gendered beings, and they were uncomfortable if a girl's behavior seemed too boyish or if a boy's taste in clothes or toys was too girly.[8] In a similar vein, Fine quotes some parents explaining the compromise they made when their son begged them for a Barbie doll: they bought him a NASCAR Barbie.[9]

It is not hard to sympathize with parents like these, who are caught between their desire for the world to be different and their obligation to ensure their children can thrive in the world as it currently exists. The resulting mixed messages become part of the puzzle that children themselves have to solve. Davies emphasizes that even preschoolers are actively engaged in the process of gender socialization—they are not just passive recipients of adult instruction. And the adults who care for them are not the only source of the knowledge they bring to bear on the task. By the time Davies met them, her young subjects had already developed a range of roles both inside and outside the family: they were pupils at preschool, members of child peer groups, and consumers of mass media and of products like food, clothes, and toys. In all these capacities, they were absorbing information about what it meant to be a girl or a boy.[10]

This learning process has been documented in observational diaries kept by feminist parents. In the 1980s the German lawyer and feminist Marianne Grabrucker published a detailed record of the first three years in the life of her daughter, Anneli, paying attention to all the ways in which relatives, friends, and strangers instructed the little girl in the rules of gender-appropriate behavior and rewarded her for performing femininity—for instance, complimenting her on looking pretty or praising her for being helpful and for deferring to the boys she played with.[11] Inspired by this example, in 2011 the British journalists Ros Ball and James Millar set up a Twitter account, @GenderDiary, in which they reflected on their experiences as parents of a girl and a boy.[12] They noticed systematic differences in the way their two children were treated and talked about as they went through the same developmental stages. For instance, when they took their baby son (the younger of the two) to the clinic, staff often commented positively on how big he was. He wasn't any bigger than his sister had been at his age, but his size was remarked on more often than hers had been. Ball and Millar also realized that when the word "big" was applied to their daughter it was more likely to refer to her "grown-up" behavior than to her physical size. Largeness is seen as a neutral or positive quality in boys but a negative one in girls. This norm is even reflected in the construction of clothing for young children. Not only are girls' and boys' clothes generally distinguished by their surface style, many brands also produce girls' clothes that are smaller than the clothes they sell for boys, beginning at an age when there are still no significant sex differences in average height or weight.

When people cite the failure of nonsexist parenting as evidence that nature trumps nurture, feminists reply that they are underestimating not only the effects of parents' subconsciously held beliefs, but also the strength of all the other cultural influences that affect children's development, and that could only be prevented from doing so if parents denied their children a normal life (no school, no friends, no TV or internet, and no mass-produced clothes and toys). Some parents have undertaken very radical experiments: in 2011, for example, a Canadian couple announced their intention to raise their youngest child, Storm (whose sex they declined to reveal), "gender neutrally."[13] In pursuit of this goal they chose to move outside the cultural mainstream and homeschool their three children. For most parents, however, this is not a practical option, and it also has political limitations in that it is an individual solution to a social problem. To address that problem on a larger scale, it is necessary to campaign for change within the mainstream.

Numerous campaigns of this kind were set up by parents in the 1970s, and they are making something of a comeback. In 2012, a discussion on the British online parenting forum Mumsnet prompted activists to organize a campaign, called Let Toys Be Toys, that aims to persuade manufacturers and retailers to stop labeling toys by gender. Producers of entertainment for children have also been responsive to criticisms about gender stereotyping. Disney, for example, has made deliberate efforts to create more assertive female protagonists in recent animated features like *Brave* and *Frozen*—though research shows that male characters still get more speaking time overall than female ones,[14] and the new generation of princesses still tend to represent a narrowly conventional notion of feminine attractiveness (typically white, youthful, and slender, with long hair and big eyes). Although they are animations rather than actual people, critics point out that the characteristics of their two-dimensional bodies are only exaggerated versions of what real girls and women are told they should aspire to.

This aspect of the social construction of femininity has prompted criticism throughout feminism's history. In chapter 2 I quoted Mary Wollstonecraft's complaint, made in the 1790s, that women were encouraged to perfect their bodies rather than their minds. The first-wave feminists who followed Wollstonecraft also criticized the emphasis placed on women's appearance and the extremely restrictive dress codes that went along with that emphasis. They particularly deplored the fashion for corsets, which were laced tightly to produce an unnaturally small waist and were worn with heavy petticoats and cumbersome skirts. In the United States in 1849 Amelia Bloomer introduced an alternative of her own invention—the Bloomer outfit, a sort of pantaloons-and-tunic combination; in Britain in the 1880s the Rational Dress Society also championed split pants, in part to allow women to participate more easily in the increasingly popular activity of bicycling. Though inevitably they were accused of wanting to destroy natural sex differences, these reformers were actually criticizing the artificiality of Victorian femininity. There was nothing natural about corsets and crinolines.

The Women's Liberation Movement that emerged during the 1960s also wanted to liberate women from oppressive and unrealistic standards of beauty and from the idea that a woman's worth was determined by her ability to produce herself as a desirable object for men's consumption. Some of the movement's earliest and most visible actions were protests against beauty pageants, where women contestants were, as the protestors saw it, paraded like cattle at a market. Like their nineteenth-century predecessors, these feminists objected to fashions that restricted women's freedom of movement or caused chronic physical discomfort (for instance, girdles and high-heeled shoes); but they were equally if not more concerned with the psychological damage inflicted on women by the pressure to perfect their appearance. This concern became even stronger in the 1990s, when commentators pointed to the rising incidence of eating disorders and the growth in demand for cosmetic surgery as signs that all was not well with the generation of women who had grown up with equal rights. "The more legal and material hindrances women have broken through," wrote Naomi Wolf in her book *The Beauty Myth*, "the more strictly and heavily and cruelly images of female beauty have come to weigh upon us."[15]

The philosopher Heather Widdows believes that the pressure on women to conform to exacting beauty standards—or, as she calls them, "beauty demands"—has become even more extreme since 1990. The same standards are increasingly applied to women globally, and the pressure to meet them lasts longer, beginning well before puberty and continuing long after menopause. Achieving the desired look requires both effort and technological assistance: the ideal woman is supposed to be young or young looking, thin or slim, golden skinned (a norm that requires most Black women to lighten their skin and white women to tan theirs), with a body that is firm, smooth, and almost entirely hairless. Desirable facial features include prominent cheekbones and large eyes—a demand that has made eye-lift surgery increasingly common in parts of Asia. Widdows notes that meeting these expectations is presented as a moral imperative: you "owe it to yourself" not to "let yourself go"; you should "make the best of yourself" "because you're worth it." Failure to measure up to the ideal is thus experienced by many women as a moral weakness, a judgment not only on their physical worth but also on their character.[16]

Some feminists might say that Widdows's own attitude is moralistic and judgmental, denying women's status as autonomous agents who can decide for themselves what is in their best interests. If we oppose attempts to tell women what they can or can't do with their reproductive organs, why is it acceptable to tell them what they should or shouldn't do with other parts of their bodies? In the immortal words of the singer Cher, "if I want to put my tits on my back, it's nobody's business but my own." Once again, though, the counterargument is that our choices are not made in a vacuum but in response to social pressures that individuals can neither control nor disregard. There are clear rewards for complying with the norms that define an acceptably feminine appearance, and clear penalties for noncompliance. For instance, studies show employers are more likely to hire, promote, and offer higher salaries to "attractive" women (and men too, but the effect is usually larger for women).[17] This system of value is something most of us will have internalized long before we are able to make consequential life decisions. Appearance-based discrimination has been observed among children as young as three: they judge peers with certain physical characteristics (like being fat) less desirable as friends and playmates.[18] If the choices we make as adults are shaped by beliefs and desires formed so early in life, can these choices really be regarded as free?

Questions about agency, choice, and freedom become especially fraught in relation to body size and weight—an aspect of women's appearance that, in contemporary Western societies, is perhaps more heavily policed than any other. Fatness is typically understood as the result of an abnegation of agency: fat people are endlessly exhorted to become slim by "controlling themselves" or making "better choices." But apart from being censorious, this view fails to capture the complexity of women's stories. In her memoir *Hunger*, Roxane Gay, who is over six feet tall and at her heaviest weighed 577 pounds, recalls that she first began to gain weight after being raped by a group of boys when she was twelve. In the aftermath of this traumatic experience, she explains, "I began eating to change my body. I was wilful in this. . . . I thought that if my body became repulsive, I could keep men away."[19] Here Gay makes an unambiguous claim to agency: she stresses that her eating was not a habit she unwittingly fell into but something she consciously chose to do. Her desire to change her body, though, arose under conditions that were not of her choosing. Women and girls do not choose to be vulnerable to sexual violence, but that vulnerability is one factor that may affect their relationships with their bodies.

Women's feelings about their bodies are also influenced by powerful industries with a vested interest in encouraging insecurity. The argument that complying with beauty demands is a woman's "choice" echoes the beauty industry's own protestations that it is only giving the customer what she wants, when, in fact, like other branches of consumer capitalism, it has a long history of creating new needs, desires, and anxieties that it can then exploit to generate more profits. (Did anyone worry about "feminine freshness" or "free radicals" before advertising brought these things to their attention?) In the global South, the desires and anxieties being exploited are also bound up with the history of colonialism and racism. Corporations based in Europe and North America have flooded the markets of Africa, Asia, and Latin America with skin-lightening preparations that do not meet the safety standards of the rich world; some are sufficiently toxic to put regular users at increased risk of developing cancers, neurological problems, and kidney disease. Even when they are not physically toxic, these products reinforce the toxic effects of racism, which is responsible for creating the hierarchy of value in which fair skin is preferred to dark skin.[20]

The negative effects of femininity on women have received critical attention during every wave of feminism, but there has always been another strand in feminist thinking that insists there is more to femininity than subordination. Traditionally female activities and rituals can be a source of pleasure, providing outlets for women's creativity and opportunities for female bonding; feminine qualities like empathy and nurturance are valuable and should be celebrated. One recently influential defense of femininity has been offered by the trans feminist Julia Serano, who criticizes feminism for reproducing the preference of patriarchal cultures for masculinity.[21] She points out that while feminism has made masculine qualities and activities more acceptable for women and girls, the reverse has not happened: our culture remains deeply uncomfortable with any display of femininity in men or boys. The discussion of nonsexist parenting earlier in this chapter offers support for this observation. Parents may be happy for their daughters to climb trees and build model spaceships, but many are more ambivalent about their sons' requests for Barbie dolls.

However, other feminists might give a different account of what's ultimately behind this difference. Parents who discourage certain interests and behaviors in boys may be motivated less by a prejudice against femininity, and more by their awareness that an insufficiently masculine boy or man is potentially a target for other men's violence. This male-on-male gender policing serves to defend the hierarchical system that requires men to behave not just differently from women, but in a way that enacts and symbolizes their dominance. Women who refuse to perform femininity are rebels, but men who flout the norms of masculinity are traitors, and the severity of the punishment reflects that.

As I noted in chapter 1, male dominance is a pervasive and complex phenomenon with very deep historical roots, and it is hardly surprising if feminism has not yet eliminated it. That does not mean it is a law of nature and that resistance to it is futile, nor does it mean that nothing has been achieved. In some communities, in some respects, the norms of femininity and masculinity have become considerably less rigid since the 1960s. But it could also be argued that some norms, like those relating to women's physical appearance, have become *more* rigid and more negative in their effects. In the next chapter I consider feminist approaches to another area of experience where change has been real but also partial, and not always unequivocally positive: sex.

5

Sex

The publishing sensation of 2012 was E. L. James's *Fifty Shades of Grey*, an erotic novel by a previously unknown author that chronicled the relationship between Christian Grey, a billionaire "dom" (the sexually dominant partner in bondage and discipline and sadomasochism, or BDSM), and Anastasia Steele, a young college graduate who is still a virgin when the two first meet.[1] The book was the first volume in a trilogy, by the end of which the couple are married with a child. Despite the trappings of "kink" (chains, whips, spanking), it is in essence a conventional heterosexual romance. However, it was the kink aspect that made *Fifty Shades* a cultural phenomenon, prompting pundits of all kinds to ask what its extraordinary appeal to women readers said about the condition of women in the twenty-first century. Did it say, for instance, that feminism has not changed the eternal truth that girls just wanna be dominated by older, richer, more powerful men? Or do today's women get pleasure from fantasies of female powerlessness precisely because they are now, in reality, so powerful? Was the popularity of these books (which spawned a whole genre, dubbed "mommy porn" by the media) a sign that women have been liberated to explore their own desires without shame, or was it worrisome evidence of their continued susceptibility to representations that make violence against women sexy?

These questions divided feminist commentators, though they were more or less united in hating the books. Whereas some argued that relationships based on male dominance and female submission are inherently problematic, others, while agreeing that *Fifty Shades* was problematic, maintained that the trouble was its misrepresentation of BDSM, which is based on a contract between equal partners, whereas Ana in the book is not Christian's equal. One commenter who took this view declared herself "fully in support of anyone doing whatever (safe, consensual) thing they want to do to get themselves off. Feminists for Orgasms!" But others criticized this kind of "orgasm politics" for taking no account of the way sexual desires are shaped by the social and political context. "Women cope with male violence and oppression," wrote one, "by eroticizing male dominance."[2]

The debate about *Fifty Shades* is one recent instance of a larger debate about sex that has gone on, in some form or other, throughout the history of feminism. As Carole Vance wrote in 1984, sex for women is "simultaneously a domain of restriction, repression and danger, as well as a domain of exploration, pleasure and agency."[3] If feminists focus only on the "pleasure" side, they risk ignoring the reality of male violence and oppression, but if they focus only on the "danger" side, they risk ignoring women's experience of sex as something actively desired and enjoyed. Few feminists would dispute that these two dimensions exist, and that feminism must address them both. But feminists have not agreed on what the balance between the two should be, and on some issues there are deep divisions between those who describe their position as "sex-positive" (like the "Feminists for Orgasms!" writer) and those who put more emphasis on the way sex becomes, in patriarchal societies, a site of exploitation and abuse.

Historians of the first wave generally agree that feminist discussions of sex in the nineteenth and early twentieth centuries were dominated by the impulse to protect women from sexual danger and to reform "the beast in man," though there were some feminists who campaigned for women's access to birth control, abortion, sex education, and the freedom to have sex outside marriage.[4] The second wave, however, took sexual politics in a new direction. Emerging in the late 1960s, the early Women's Liberation Movement drew energy and inspiration from a counterculture that rebelled against the sexual conservatism of mainstream postwar society, rejecting its attempts to confine sex within the limits of bourgeois marriage and reproduction. This sexual revolution was part of a utopian political project: not only was having more, freer sex considered positive in itself, it was also thought of as a means to other positive political ends (as is suggested by slogans like "make love, not war"). For women, sexual freedom had particularly radical implications, because sex had so often been the ground on which women's freedom was restricted. The risks and punishments associated with sexual activity outside marriage were greater for women than for men: not only a woman's sexual behavior, but all her public behavior (what she did, where she went, who she met) had to be policed to avoid damaging her all-important reputation. Lynne Segal, herself a member of the generation that rebelled against these restrictions, says that for the women of the early second wave, "women's rights to sexual pleasure and fulfilment, on their own terms, symbolized their rights to autonomy and selfhood."[5] It was not, in other words, just about sex.

But sex was certainly part of what it was about. At the same time their behavior was being policed to ward off the ever-present threat that they would engage in illicit sex, women were also being informed by medical and other experts that they were by nature less interested in sex than men, as well as naturally passive and inclined to monogamy (whereas men were naturally promiscuous). Feminists were quick to point out the contradictions in this view of female sexuality, and keen to demonstrate its inaccuracy. One recurring theme in early second-wave writing was the exploration, and celebration, of all the desires women were not supposed to have—whether for the kind of anonymous, commitment-free heterosexual encounter that the heroine of Erica Jong's 1973 novel *Fear of Flying* called "the zipless fuck" or for sexual relationships with other women.

Another recurring theme, though, was the failure of the sexual revolution to deliver pleasure and fulfillment on women's terms. In a widely read short paper entitled "The Myth of the Vaginal Orgasm," Anne Koedt pointed out that the work of the sexologists William H. Masters and Virginia E. Johnson, which had been published in the mid-1960s, confirmed that the female orgasm originates in the clitoris.[6] Yet psychoanalysts, therapists, and purveyors of popular advice continued to maintain that a "mature" woman who had fully accepted her own femininity could and should experience orgasm through penis-in-vagina intercourse. Koedt suggested that what kept this idea in circulation, despite its being contradicted by both science and experience, was the fact that it served men's interests. Women had been "defined sexually in terms of what pleases men," and if they didn't find intercourse satisfying they were told there was something wrong with them. The way forward, Koedt declared, was to "create new guidelines which take into account mutual sexual enjoyment. . . . We must demand that if certain sexual positions now defined as 'standard' are not mutually conducive to orgasm, they no longer be defined as standard."

The problem Koedt and her contemporaries identified has still not been solved. As recently as 2016, the writer Peggy Orenstein noted in her book *Girls and Sex* that pleasure was treated as a given for boys but an afterthought for girls. This rule extended beyond intercourse: the girls she interviewed told her that they routinely performed oral sex, and that boys expected this; but the favor was very rarely returned, and most girls did not question the lack of reciprocity. Orenstein suggests that this issue could be addressed through better sex education. The information young people currently receive tends to be focused on bodily mechanics, and in the case of the female body the emphasis is often more on reproduction than sex, leaving no space to talk about desires, feelings, and relationships. Both at school and at home, girls are more likely to be warned about the dangers of sex (pregnancy, disease, and rape) than engaged in a discussion of its pleasures. For the many young Americans whose school sex-education program is abstinence based, the only advice they get is "don't."[7] And like many contemporary commentators, Orenstein worries about the source many young people are turning to instead: pornography.[8]

Whether pornography represents pleasure or danger is one of the questions that divide feminists most starkly. There are long-standing arguments between those who see its representation of sex as an incitement to real-world sexual violence and abuse ("porn is the theory, rape is the practice") and those who see it as a valuable resource, enabling people—especially women and members of sexual minorities—to explore their desires, learn about their bodies, and see themselves represented as sexual beings. Feminists who take the latter view may acknowledge that women are not well served by most commercial pornography, which is designed for heterosexual men. They argue, however, that the answer is not to oppose pornography as such but rather to exploit its potential by demanding, or producing, alternatives that are less male centered and sexist. They also worry that opposition to porn puts feminists on the same side as religious conservatives, who would like to censor all representations of sex, not to mention all real-world expressions of sexuality that do not meet their moral standards. In response, antiporn feminists say that their overriding concern is not with sexual morality as conservatives understand it but with the abuse of women, children, and men both inside the pornography industry and in the wider society that consumes its products.

These arguments featured prominently in the feminist "sex wars" of the 1980s and reemerged later on, when all kinds of pornography became easily accessible online. Research suggests that while men continue to consume more porn than women, both sexes are seeing more of it than they did in the 1980s and are encountering it at younger ages.[9] At the same time, other elements of what used to be a hidden and stigmatized subculture have now been brought into the cultural mainstream. Strip joints have been rebranded as gentlemen's clubs, and pole dancing is pitched to women as a sexy way of keeping fit. Together these trends represent what some feminists call porn culture, meaning not simply a culture where porn exists but one where it is normalized and ubiquitous.[10] And some feminists argue that the rise of porn culture is linked to the rise of rape culture—again, not just a culture where rape exists, but a culture that normalizes and enables it.[11]

It might seem strange to talk about the culture "enabling" something that the law defines as a crime second only to murder. But most rape prosecutions do not end in a conviction, and many incidents are not prosecuted or even reported because cultural myths and stereotypes (like "once they're aroused men can't help themselves," and "women say no when they don't mean it") stop many people from seeing rape as real unless it happens at knifepoint in a dark alley. The same myths also prompt people to look for reasons to blame the victim rather than the perpetrator ("she was asking for it by getting drunk/flirting/wearing those clothes," or "she's lying because she's ashamed/vengeful/attention seeking"). While many factors contribute to the prevalence of rape myths, some feminist campaigners believe that porn culture is one. You don't have to believe that porn directly causes rape to see it as one repository of the beliefs and attitudes that enable so many men to rape with impunity. As in the 1980s, though, other feminists reject this argument, insisting that it is possible, and indeed necessary, to oppose rape and rape culture while also asserting women's right to be actively and visibly sexual. This is the attitude expressed in the recent phenomenon of "slutwalks," antirape protests at which some women wear stereotypically sexy clothes to contest the idea that women who dress or behave in certain ways are inviting or provoking sexual violence. The first slutwalk was organized in 2011 after a police officer in Toronto told a group of students they should "avoid dressing like sluts" for their own safety.

Arguments about the effects of porn culture do not all focus on whether it contributes to the prevalence of rape. Peggy Orenstein, for instance, is more concerned that it reinforces the focus on what is pleasurable for men, who are the target audience for most pornography, within consensual sexual relationships. This concern is not confined to older feminists who did not grow up with the culture they criticize. In 2015 a woman posted anonymously on Twitter:

"I'm 23. Mine is the first generation to be exposed to online porn from a young age. We learnt what sex is from watching strangers on the internet." She went on to list various porn-inspired things her male sexual partners had done without asking her (such as pulling her hair and ejaculating on her face), pressured her into doing despite her reluctance (such as having anal sex), or criticized her for refusing to do (such as participating in group sex). None of these were things she herself desired, yet she recalls that "on every single occasion I felt guilty for not being a 'cool girl.' I was letting him down. I was a prude."

This writer is suggesting that porn culture has brought with it new expectations of female heterosexual performance that women like herself feel inadequate if they do not meet. The distinction she makes between "cool girls" and "prudes" may look completely different from the more traditional one between "nice girls" and "sluts," but it functions in a similar way: in both cases, the fear of being on the wrong side of the line spurs women to police their own behavior. Rather than liberating women to pursue sexual pleasure on their own terms, porn culture just replaces one oppressive standard ("nice girls don't") with another ("cool girls do whatever men want"). But as ever, there are other feminists who say that they do find pleasure and fulfillment in the sexual practices that the Twitter writer rejects, and that pornography has enhanced their experience by opening up new erotic possibilities.

Clearly, women's sexual desires vary. But in dealing with that reality, as Lisa Downing, a feminist scholar who describes her approach as "neither sex-positive nor sex-negative, but *sex-critical*," has argued, feminist discussions often become polarized between two positions. One, channeling the utopian spirit of the sexual revolution, holds that sex is good in and of itself, and any kind of sex that any woman finds pleasurable must automatically be liberating and politically progressive. The other maintains that (hetero)sex under patriarchy is inherently oppressive, and any pleasure women derive from it must be considered suspect. Downing's own view is that both these arguments are too simple, and that "all forms of sexuality and all sexual representations should be equally susceptible to critical thinking and interrogation."[12]

What feminist opponents of porn culture criticize is not just pornography but the mainstreaming of the sex industry more generally. This raises questions not only about women's position as consumers of the industry's products, but also about their involvement in it as sex workers, an umbrella term that covers a range of occupations from glamour modeling and stripping to prostitution, the direct sale of sexual services. This is another issue on which feminists are deeply divided. Is selling sex just a job like any other, problematic only insofar as it is criminalized and socially stigmatized, or is it a form of sexual exploitation which will always be incompatible with the principles of sexual equality and justice?

Feminist debates on prostitution have a long history. Many American feminists in the nineteenth and early twentieth centuries campaigned against prostitution, but as the historian Ruth Rosen explains, their motivations were often somewhat different from those of the conservatives who dominated the larger reform movement. Whereas conservatives saw the prostitute as immoral and disruptive, feminists were more likely to regard her as "the quintessential symbol of the sexual and economic exploitation of women."[13] Their opposition to prostitution went along with their opposition to the sexual double standard, which required "respectable" women to be chaste while condoning promiscuity in men—and at the same time condemning the women, including prostitutes, who supplied men's demand for extramarital sex. Without male demand there would be no prostitution, but the stigma fell only on the women involved. Feminists who held this view saw the eradication of prostitution as a way to elevate the status of women in general. But as Rosen also notes, they often supported policies that in practice did nothing to help women working in prostitution: on the contrary, the effect was often to expose prostitutes, or poor women suspected of working as prostitutes, to increased harassment by the authorities.

In some cases feminists did protest against this kind of harassment. In Britain in the late 1860s, there was a national feminist-led campaign to repeal the Contagious Diseases Acts, which allowed the police in military garrison towns to arrest any woman suspected of being a "common prostitute" and force her to submit to a medical inspection. If she refused she could be imprisoned, and if she was found to have an infection she could be involuntarily confined to a hospital. The campaign's manifesto denounced the law for giving official sanction to the double standard, discriminating against its targets on the basis of their sex and class, denying them basic rights, and subjecting them to a degrading procedure that might well be called instrumental rape. Though they could be censorious about prostitution, these campaigners, most of whom belonged to a privileged social class, understood that women's involvement in it was driven by economic need. In a society that severely restricted women's access to other forms of work, selling sex was often "the best-paid industry." Some of the campaigners also understood that the contempt with which prostitutes were treated was an overt expression of the same cultural misogyny whose more genteel forms also permeated their own relationships with men.[14]

Feminists who oppose prostitution today have a similar

analysis of its workings as an economic and social institution.[15] They argue that the existence of a market where
men can buy sexual consent (that is, pay for sexual acts that
the other party would not choose to perform without pay-
ment) both reflects and reinforces inequality between the
sexes, and it undermines the principle that sex should be
an exchange based on mutual desire. Many feminists who
make these arguments are supporters of the Nordic model
(so called because it was pioneered in Sweden and subsequently adopted in Norway and Iceland), which prohibits
the purchase of sexual services while decriminalizing the
act of selling them. The law is intended both to transfer
the legal sanctions associated with commercial sex from
prostitutes (mainly women) to sex buyers (overwhelmingly
men) and to reduce the overall demand. The model also
includes provisions to support those involved in prostitution and enable them, if they wish, to move out of it.

Other feminists, however, argue that the Nordic model
is based on moralistic and patronizing attitudes to women
who sell sex, and that a more progressive approach would
recognize that "sex work is work." Selling sex is in principle
no different from, say, giving beauty treatments, which may
also require intimate contact between worker and client, or
cleaning toilets, which also involves dealing with strangers'
bodily effluvia. Feminists who take this view often make
the same observation I made in chapter 3, that doing things
you don't enjoy in exchange for the money you need to pay
your bills is the lot of most of the world's working women.
If a woman sees prostitution as a rational economic choice,
what right has anyone else to criticize her, let alone campaign for measures that will put her out of a job? From this
perspective, feminists should support sex workers by campaigning for improvements in their working conditions—
and especially for the decriminalization or legalization of

prostitution (the difference between the two is that legalized prostitution is regulated by the state). They point out that women engaged in an illegal activity cannot easily take action to reduce the risks involved: they will hesitate to report abusive men to the police or to complain about working practices that compromise their health and safety. If the selling of sex were put on the same footing as the selling of any other service, it would make women safer, reduce the stigma attached to their occupation, and open up opportunities for them to take control of their working lives. They could set up small businesses or cooperatives with other women instead of depending on pimps and organized criminals, who are powerful players in the illegal trade.

Their opponents respond that the risks involved in selling sex cannot be reduced to an acceptable level, because so many of them arise from the nature of the job rather than its legal status. The most serious occupational hazard of prostitution is being assaulted or even killed by a buyer during the private sexual encounter that is central to the business, and this hazard exists whether prostitution is legal or illegal. Campaigners also say that in countries with legalized prostitution, like Germany and the Netherlands, the promised benefits for women have not materialized. Instead the industry has been freed to reorganize along neoliberal capitalist lines, with wealthy investors and entrepreneurs, not workers, reaping the financial rewards. Women selling sex in Germany's legalized megabrothels have not become employees with rights and benefits, let alone co-owners and managers; rather, they are treated as self-employed contractors, paying the management a fee for each shift they work, which means they must service several men before they start earning money for themselves.

It is not only in the commercial sex trade that women may exchange sex for money or other benefits. Both first-

and early second-wave feminists sometimes argued that marriage was only a legal and respectable form of prostitution, in which wives provided sexual and domestic services to their husbands in exchange for their financial support. Under the law as it stood in the nineteenth century and for most of the twentieth, wives could not withhold consent to sex: a husband's conjugal rights were treated as an integral part of the marriage contract. The first prosecution of a man for raping his wife while they were living together did not take place in the United States until 1978, and marital rape did not become a crime in all fifty states until 1993. Even now, the idea of sex as a tradable commodity continues to influence everyday understandings of the relationship between women and men. Several former prostitutes told author and feminist activist Kat Banyard that they had understood sex as their most valuable asset long before they began to sell it. One woman explained that from an early age she had seen her sexuality as "a thing men wanted from me and which I had to give them to feel that I was worth something." Another said her experience had taught her that as a woman "your primary source of power is your sexual power."[16]

The same assumptions have been visible in debates prompted by recent revelations about sexual harassment and exploitation in the entertainment industry. Not only did men like Harvey Weinstein operate on the assumption that women who wanted to advance their careers would be willing to offer sexual favors in return, critics of #MeToo (including Brigitte Bardot, the actor Ian McKellen, and the singer Morrissey) have suggested that some alleged cases of coercion were really consensual exchanges of sex for other benefits. There is still a widespread belief that sex, for women, is not an end in itself but largely a means to some other end, like power, status, wealth, or fame. That is also the received wisdom of the men's rights movement, particularly among men who call themselves incels (involuntarily celibate).[17] These men resent women for allegedly reserving their sexual favors for "alpha males" and denying lower-status men the sex to which they think they are entitled. Absent from this whole discourse is the idea that women might desire sex for its own sake or that their sexuality might not be geared entirely to pleasing men.

While some feminists have put their energies into creating more equal ways for men and women to relate to each another sexually, others have advocated alternatives to heterosexuality. One alternative is refusing sex entirely. There was once a group of American radical feminists who called themselves Women against Sex and whose manifesto proclaimed that "there is no way out of the practice of sexuality except *out*."[18] People who today identify as asexual are not usually motivated by the same analysis, but they do arguably represent a challenge to the prevailing assumption that sexuality and sexual activity are essential for human flourishing. Other feminists have viewed sexual (and other intimate) relationships between women as a positive, and politically radical, alternative to heterosexuality. The French feminist writer Monique Wittig, for instance, maintained that a lesbian is not a woman; she did not mean that lesbians are not female, but rather that they exist outside the system of heterosexual exchange that defines "women" as a social category.[19]

In 1980, in an article entitled "Compulsory Heterosexuality and Lesbian Existence," the poet Adrienne Rich argued that heterosexuality should be seen not simply as a choice or a natural inclination but as a political institution whose dictates most women historically had little choice but to comply with. Though prohibitions on homosexuality applied to both sexes, the pressure to engage in heterosexual relationships (ruling out not only lesbianism but also celibacy) bore especially heavily on women because of their economic dependence on marriage. Rich asked her readers to consider the possibility that this pressure, and the persecution of women who resisted it, reflected a well-founded fear that if they were truly free to choose, many women would choose each other.[20]

Rich's article was written to challenge what she saw as the marginalization of lesbians and lesbianism in the theory and practice of second-wave feminism. Women who defined themselves as lesbians before the late 1960s initially had an uneasy relationship with the new feminist movement, which many saw as homophobic—and not without reason. Betty Friedan, who led the National Organization for Women (NOW), once described lesbians as a "lavender menace" whose visibility in the movement would undermine mainstream support for its objectives.[21] Some lesbians continued to feel that the Gay Liberation Movement was more relevant to their concerns, while others identified with the Women's Liberation Movement. Black lesbian feminists also had links to Black political organizations: as the Combahee River Collective pointed out in a 1977 statement, its commitment to fighting racism as well as sexism precluded the total separation from men that some white lesbian feminists advocated.[22] The women who formed the collective, however, did so because they did not feel their concerns were fully represented by any of the organizations they had previously belonged to. They broke away from the National Black Feminist Organization (NBFO) in part because it shared NOW's ambivalence about the visibility of lesbians in the movement. As the 1977 statement explains, while the collective shared the NBFO's central concern with the combined sexism and racism faced by Black women, it was not willing to put the issue of sexuality to one side: "We are actively committed to struggling against racial, sexual, heterosexual, and class oppression, and see as our particular task the development of integrated analysis and practice based upon the fact that the major systems of oppression are interlocking."[23] Though the term was not yet in use in 1977, this is a clear commitment to what we would now call intersectional analysis. And by including heterosexism among the intersecting oppressions members saw as relevant to their situation, the Combahee River Collective took a position that few feminist organizations, whether Black or white, could be relied on to support at the time.

The feminism of the late 1960s and 1970s did not just bring about changes in women's legal status and their social roles; for many women, it also changed their personal relationships and their understanding of who they were. Sex and sexuality were part of this process: some women who had previously thought of themselves as heterosexual were led by their involvement with feminism to discover the erotic potential of relationships between women and to redefine themselves as lesbians. The present is arguably another time in which identities and desires are being reshaped by new social and cultural developments. One indication of this shift, it has been suggested, is that young women are turning away from lesbianism and toward what they see as the more inclusive or fluid identity designated by the label "queer."[24] Once a common insult aimed at homosexuals, in the "reclaimed" usage that emerged from the queer theory and activism of the 1980s and 1990s, "queer" does not refer exclusively to gay men and lesbians. Rather it includes all sexual preferences and practices that challenge "heteronormativity," the privileging of a form of heterosexuality that is monogamous, procreative, based on traditional gender roles, and favoring conventional erotic practices. So, if more women are indeed identifying as queer rather than lesbian, the question arises whether this is just a shift in terminology (they're still doing the same things with the same people, but under a different label), or whether it indicates a more radical change in the social organization of sexuality. This is a complicated question, but one answer is hinted at by a commentator who observed that "against the increasingly colorful backdrop of gender diversity, a binary label like 'gay' or 'lesbian' starts to feel somewhat stale and stodgy."[25] Current shifts in our ways of talking, thinking about, and maybe even doing sex are closely connected to changing ideas about gender identity—a subject I will return to in the final chapter.

Meanwhile, since this chapter has had much to say about the divisions among feminists on the subject of sex, I will conclude by saying something about what unites them. What makes all the views I have been considering feminist, however different they are from one another, is the assertion that women are, and should be treated as, autonomous sexual subjects, not objects to be used for others' pleasure and profit. Women should be free to express their sexuality without being defined exclusively in sexual terms. Their desires should matter, and their boundaries should be respected. As basic as these demands might seem, they are radical demands even now.

6

Culture

The critic Camille Paglia once declared that "if civilization had been left in female hands, we would still be living in grass huts."[1] This was not an original thought. Paglia was recycling the old idea that men are the creators of culture—using that word not in its anthropological sense of "a whole way of life," but as an umbrella term for the most valued products of human intellect and creativity—because of their drive to transcend and control the forces of nature. Women, meanwhile, remain tethered to nature, using their creative energies not in the pursuit of knowledge, truth, and beauty but in the natural process of reproduction.

In *The Descent of Man*, his major work on human evolution, Charles Darwin pondered the evidence of women's cultural inferiority. "If two lists were made of the most eminent men and women in poetry, painting, sculpture, music, history, science and philosophy," he mused, "the two lists would not bear comparison." He concluded that the difference must have a biological cause: men were innately endowed with "a higher standard of mental power."[2] That was also the view of Cesare Lombroso, the nineteenth-century Italian physician and criminologist who published a book-length study entitled *L'Uomo di Genio* (*The Man of Genius*). Chapter 3 of the book includes the section "Influence of Sex," which begins by observing that "in the history of genius women have but a small place." On the next page we discover that even this is an overstatement: the few female candidates for the title of genius all turn out to have "something virile about them." Lombroso concludes with the remark that "there are no women of genius: the women of genius are men."[3]

Absurd though we may find this logic, the basic argument remains a cliché of popular antifeminism. If women are really equal to men, people say, where is the female Leonardo, Shakespeare, or Mozart? Which female philosopher or political thinker has had the influence of Confucius, Plato, or Marx? Why are there so few female Nobel laureates, and how do we explain the fact that only one woman (the late Maryam Mirzakhani) has ever won the prestigious Fields Medal for mathematics? These questions have been asked throughout feminism's history; in this chapter I will consider some of the answers feminists have given, and more generally how they have theorized women's relationship to art, knowledge, and creativity. (I should acknowledge here that the discussion will focus on Western and European cultural traditions. These are not, of course, the only traditions of interest, and feminist accounts of women's place within them should not be taken as universal statements about the relationship of all women to all traditions.)

The first-wave feminists who were Darwin's contemporaries did not generally dispute that women's intellectual and artistic achievements were fewer and less distinguished than those of "the most eminent men." What they did dispute, however, was that this state of affairs was natural and immutable. Many feminists were enthusiastic supporters of Darwin, because the idea that every species developed through a continuous process of adaptation seemed to support their belief that women, if given the opportunity, were capable of developing to the same level as men. Faced with his disparaging comments in *The Descent of Man*, the

American feminist Antoinette Brown Blackwell accused Darwin of failing to follow his own logic, according to which sex differences, like all other characteristics of the human species, were in principle subject to the workings of evolution.[4]

Whether or not they used arguments drawn from evolutionary theory, feminists in the nineteenth and early twentieth centuries were in no doubt that women's contributions to culture had been limited by their subordinate status, their lack of education, and their confinement to the domestic sphere. In her 1929 essay *A Room of One's Own*, Virginia Woolf addressed the perennial "why no female Shakespeare" question by asking whether a hypothetical Judith Shakespeare, William's equally gifted sister, could have risen to the same heights as her brother in the conditions of early modern England.[5] The life story she constructs for the fictional Judith makes clear that the answer must be no. Unlike her brother, Judith is never sent to school. She does learn to read, but if her mother sees her reading she is scolded for neglecting her domestic chores. When she is seventeen her parents decide it is time to find her a husband, and she is betrothed to a local wool stapler. Horrified by the prospect of marriage, she runs away to London to seek her fortune in the theater. But the Elizabethan theater does not employ women, and the city is a dangerous place for a young woman on her own. Eventually Judith finds a male patron, but—predictably—his support has a price. Unmarried and pregnant, she takes her own life.

In Woolf's own time, the early twentieth century, women of her social class had more opportunity than Shakespeare's sister to develop their talents, but they were still not in the same position as their brothers. *A Room of One's Own* discusses a number of obstacles that stood in their way, such as inferior education, economic dependence, and the continuing expectation that they would put their roles as wives and mothers first. For less privileged women, the barriers were much higher. In her 1974 essay "In Search of Our Mothers' Gardens," Alice Walker asks, "What did it mean for a Black woman to be an artist in our grandmothers' time?" She adds, "It is a question with an answer cruel enough to stop the blood."[6] Yet as she goes on to point out, poor and uneducated Black women did not lack creativity. The talents that might, under other conditions, have produced great literature or painting or sculpture were channeled instead into oral storytelling, quilt making, or, in Walker's mother's case, gardening.

Today women are told they can do anything they put their minds to and be judged entirely on their merits; but in practice the playing field is far from level. In a 2017 lecture on women and film entitled "A Screen of One's Own," the director Susanna White looked back on her own career, retracing a route that had been full of obstacles, detours, and dead ends—though at least she reached her chosen destination, which many women in her profession still do not.[7] For the past fifteen years, equal numbers of women and men have been graduating from film school with ambitions to become feature film directors. But of those who go on to achieve their goal, the vast majority are men. Most of the features women direct are modest, low-budget productions: only 3 percent of big-budget movies are directed by women. White believes the imbalance reflects ingrained sexist assumptions that are difficult to challenge because they are rarely made explicit. It is assumed that women will find it harder to manage a large cast and crew, and that those who have families will be unwilling to work long hours—though some of the longest hours on film sets are worked by people in the costume, hair, and makeup departments, which have always been dominated by women. Another common assumption is that women can only direct certain kinds of material. White was offered her first feature after she had been nominated for an Emmy for her work on a TV miniseries about the invasion of Iraq. Nevertheless, what she was offered was a movie aimed at children. (She imagined advertisements saying "From the director of *Generation Kill*: *Nanny McPhee and the Big Bang*.") She has since directed a big-budget thriller and a historical drama. But this is still unusual: in mainstream cinema it is so rare for women directors to be able to compile a sizable body of work that most people can't even name more than a handful of them (Kathryn Bigelow, Jane Campion, Sophia Coppola).

Will those names be remembered a hundred years from now? We might hope so, but another form of cultural exclusion feminists have documented is the persistent tendency for women, even those whose talents were recognized in their own time, to be erased from the historical record. In 1970 Shulamith Firestone could answer her own question, "what about the women who have contributed directly to culture?" with the brief answer, "there aren't many."[8] But later feminist scholarship would reveal there had been more than Firestone knew. Reclaiming women's past cultural contributions became, and remains, an important goal for feminist research, not only because of the intrinsic value of their work, but also because making their achievements visible challenges the belief that "there have never been any great women Xs," which continues to discourage and exclude women in the present.

In the realm of science, feminist scholarship has called attention to a number of accomplished women: the eighteenth-century astronomer Caroline Herschel; the nineteenth-century fossil collector and paleontologist Mary Anning; the early twentieth-century American biologist Nettie Stevens, who identified the role of the X and

Y chromosomes in sex determination; the midcentury physicist Lise Meitner, who, with Otto Hahn, discovered nuclear fission; the astrophysicist Jocelyn Bell Burnell, who discovered pulsars as a PhD student in the 1960s; and the NASA mathematician Katherine Johnson, whose story was told in the 2016 film *Hidden Figures*. In a field of artistic endeavor whose canonical figures are almost without exception male—musical composition in the Western classical tradition—scholarship has revealed a wealth of female talent going back centuries. In *Sounds and Sweet Airs: The Forgotten Women of Classical Music*, Anna Beer discusses not only some women whose names we know because of their connection to a famous male composer (like Fanny Hensel, who was Felix Mendelssohn's sister, and Clara Wieck, who married Robert Schumann), but also some less familiar examples, such as Francesca Caccini, who worked as a court composer in Renaissance Florence; Elisabeth Jacquet de la Guerre, the first Frenchwoman to have an opera performed; and Marianna Martines, a compatriot and contemporary of Haydn who in her own lifetime was highly regarded as a composer of sacred music.[9]

In addition to writing these women back into the record, feminists have asked how they came to be erased. In the case of the scientists, a recurring theme is the Matilda effect, a tendency to credit women's achievements to the men they work with (it was named after the American suffragist Matilda Joslyn Gage, who wrote about the phenomenon in the late nineteenth century). Neither Meitner nor Bell Burnell was honored with a Nobel Prize—not because their discoveries were overlooked, but because the Nobel committee chose to recognize only Meitner's male collaborator and Bell Burnell's male PhD supervisor. Even Marie Curie, the one female scientist almost everyone can name, was initially left out of the nomination for the 1903 Nobel Prize, which she ultimately shared with Henri Becquerel and her husband, Pierre—and she was added only after Pierre complained. The committees in these cases apparently could not imagine a male-female partnership in which the woman was an equal partner, let alone one in which she took the lead. This problem is not confined to science: Anna Beer mentions the case of Rebecca Clarke, who was awarded a prize in 1919 for a violin sonata she had composed, only for questions to be asked about whether "Rebecca Clarke" might be a pseudonym for the man who had actually composed it. It was even suggested that the man in question might be the French composer Maurice Ravel—a compliment to Clarke's abilities, but an insult to her sex.

In the arts, a common way of devaluing women's work is to relegate it to "minor" status—to say, yes, some of these women are competent, but they do not rise to the level of greatness, for their work is mediocre, derivative, trivial, sentimental, light. It has, in other words, the same inferior qualities that are often attributed to women themselves. This trope was identified by feminists early on. In 1968 the literary critic Mary Ellmann complained that "books by women are treated as though they themselves were women, and criticism embarks . . . upon an intellectual measuring of busts and hips."[10] It still seems to be impossible for women writers *not* to be read through the prism of gender, as the novelist Catherine Nichols discovered in 2015 when, as an experiment, she sent the same manuscript out to literary agents using either her own name or the name of a fictitious male alter-ego, "George." The agents who read Catherine's work praised her "lyrical" prose; George's writing, on the other hand, was commended for being "clever" and "well constructed." It was George whose writing they preferred. With seventeen expressions of interest to Catherine's two, George was, as Nichols drily remarked, "eight and a half times more successful than me at writing the same book."[11] Since all the agents had in fact read the same text, their more positive response to "George" suggests that their judgments were affected by an unconscious bias toward men.

The critic Lili Loofbourow thinks this kind of bias can be attributed at least partly to the workings of what she labels "the male glance." What she means by that term is a tendency to read women's narratives in a glancing, superficial, or inattentive way without making the effort to look for the complexity and difficulty we expect in nontrivial works of art. As an example she quotes Mark Twain's complaint that Jane Austen's novels are peopled by unlikable characters, and remarks on his failure to consider the possibility that Austen made them unlikable intentionally, to serve her larger artistic purpose. "The male glance," Loofbourow argues, "is how comedies about women become 'chick flicks.' It's how discussions of serious movies with female protagonists consign them to the unappealing stable of 'strong female characters.' It's how soap operas and reality television become synonymous with trash."[12] Of course, some works by women may indeed be trivial and trashy, lacking depth or narrative technique, but the point is that they are too often approached on the assumption that they cannot be anything else, and then read in a way that reinforces that assumption.

There are other reasons why women's art has been so persistently judged minor, many of them related to the restricted access female artists have had to the most prestigious genres and audiences. Female composers in the past were rarely able to compose symphonic works for large orchestras; female painters were often commissioned or expected to paint "female" subjects, like the domestic interiors and mother-and-child portraits we associate with the impressionists Berthe Morisot and Mary Cassatt. There is also the question of what is preserved for posterity. Francesca Caccini will always remain a little-known, minor figure because her scores have not survived to be performed and studied. And in the visual arts, as the anonymous feminist activists who call themselves Guerilla Girls have been pointing out since 1985, women's work is devalued and rendered marginal by its absence or underrepresentation in museum collections and exhibitions. One famous Guerilla Girl poster asked, "Do women have to be naked to get into the Met. Museum?" It pointed out that in the New York City Metropolitan Museum, works by women artists are greatly outnumbered by works depicting naked women.

No feminist would dispute that female artists, writers, musicians, and filmmakers deserve the same opportunities and the same recognition as their male counterparts. But some would argue that giving a few exceptional women their place in the tradition or canon that has unjustly excluded them does not address the deeper problem, which is the male centeredness of culture itself. The standards we use to judge greatness or merit, or even what counts as art or knowledge in the first place, are not neutral standards; they belong to a tradition created by men, for men, and in the image of men. As Beauvoir put it, men "describe [the world] from a point of view that is their own and that they confound with the absolute truth."[13] That's why feminists should care who holds the pen, the brush, or the camera: it is not just a question of demanding equal opportunities for individual artists who happen to be female, but also a matter of wanting the world to be represented from a different point of view—or points of view, given that "women" denotes an internally diverse category, and that even within the limited arena that exists for them to tell their stories, some women have had more space than others. Susanna White argues that women's stories matter because the way we see ourselves represented in art influences our perceptions of what is possible and desirable in life. By way of illustration she cites the first *Hunger Games* film, whose bow-and-arrow-wielding protagonist Katniss inspired a huge increase in the number of girls taking up archery. This particular example might be trivial, but the general principle is not.

Can it really be assumed, though, that simply increasing the number of representations made by women will automatically produce a different picture? Hasn't everyone's way of seeing the world, women's as well as men's, been shaped by patriarchal traditions? Firestone believed so. Discussing the work of some nineteenth-century female painters, she remarked that they "saw women through men's eyes, painted a male's idea of female."[14] For her this rendered their work inauthentic, though she recognized that they were forced into that position by the lack of any alternative, authentically female tradition. In the years after she wrote, a number of theorists and art practitioners would explore this issue in greater depth. How are women brought to see themselves and the world through male eyes? Could feminists create new traditions, and if so, what would their representations look like?

In his 1972 book *Ways of Seeing*, based on a TV series with the same title, John Berger considered how the conventions of Western representational art have both reflected and reinforced patriarchal assumptions about women's nature and social role. The most famous part of his discussion explains that in both life and art, "*men act and women appear*. Men look at women. Women watch themselves being looked at. This determines not only most relations between men and women, but also women's relation to themselves. The surveyor of woman in herself is male: the surveyed female. Thus she turns herself into an object—and most particularly an object of vision: a sight."[15] Berger illustrates this thesis with a discussion of the European tradition of nude painting. The female nude, he explains, is an object of erotic desire for a spectator who is assumed to be a heterosexual male. But in many cases the artist represents her in a way that makes her complicit in, if not responsible for, her own objectification. He might paint her with her body twisted toward the spectator, its unnatural contortion underlining her eagerness to display herself; he might paint her looking straight at the spectator, actively soliciting and taking pleasure in his desire; or he might show her admiring herself in a mirror. Berger finds this last convention especially hypocritical: "You put a mirror in her hand and called the painting 'Vanity,' thus morally condemning the woman whose nakedness you had depicted for your own pleasure."[16] The woman's body is a commodity in a transaction between men—the one who paints her and the one(s) who paid for her to be painted—but the conventions for representing her make it seem as if she is in control.

Three years after *Ways of Seeing*, the feminist filmmaker and theorist Laura Mulvey published an academic article entitled "Visual Pleasure and Narrative Cinema," in which she elaborated the concept of the male gaze.[17] This phrase is now often used to mean simply the way men look at women, but Mulvey meant something more complicated. Like Berger, she argued that the conventions of representation call on all spectators, whoever they may be, to adopt the viewpoint of a heterosexual man: to identify with the male protagonist(s) at the center of the action, and to look at the female characters in the same objectifying way they are looked at by the men on screen. In the case of narrative cinema, one key instrument for achieving this effect—making the audience look *with* the male characters and *at* the female ones—is the camera. What viewers see or pay attention to is constrained by the positioning and the movement of the camera, and typically the effect is to align the viewer's gaze with the male protagonist's point of view. For instance, the camera might show a male character looking intently at a woman, thus encouraging viewers to look with him, or it might communicate that he is looking at her by mimicking the trajectory of his gaze—panning slowly over the female character's body, say, or zooming in to show parts of her in close-up. The male gaze thus becomes the default way of looking, not just for heterosexual men but for all viewers. And this highly gendered way of looking becomes associated with the pleasure we get from the whole experience of watching films. This is another way in which women as well as men are induced to objectify the female body.

Later work from a Black or intersectional feminist perspective has emphasized that the gaze that is constructed in Western and European art is not only male but also white, racist, and colonialist.[18] Directed toward Black women, this gaze produces a distinctive form of objectification. A number of writers have examined how this worked in the case of Sarah Baartman, a Khoisan woman who was taken from South Africa to Europe in the early nineteenth century to be exhibited to paying audiences under the racist sobriquet "the Hottentot Venus." Not only in life but even after her death, when for the benefit of European "race science" her body was dissected and parts of it displayed in a museum, Baartman was literally treated as a specimen, an exemplar of the "primitive" and hypersexual African woman whose body was presented, in one scholar's words, as "a titillating curiosity, a collage of buttocks and genitalia."[19] While few Europeans today would defend this treatment, some continue to make use of the degrading iconography found in nineteenth-century images of Black women like Baartman. Those images are clearly alluded to, for instance, in Jean-Paul Goude's famous photograph of Grace Jones naked and on all fours in a cage, and more recently, of Kim Kardashian balancing a champagne glass on her buttocks (though Kardashian, who is white, wears an evening dress and gloves).

Theoretical accounts like the ones I have been discussing are intended, in the first instance, to explain how certain representations work and what they accomplish in the process. But they may also prompt experiments with alternative forms of representation. In the Belgian director Chantal Akerman's 1975 film *Jeanne Dielman, 23 Quai du Commerce, 1080 Bruxelles* (hailed by the *New York Times* as "the first masterpiece of the feminine in the history of the cinema") the protagonist, Jeanne, a single mother who supports herself and her son by selling sex to male clients in her home, is shown going about her daily routine over a period of three consecutive days. Mundane activities like making beds, washing dishes, and preparing meals are shot in real time, disrupting the usual expectation that dramatic or unexpected events will be foregrounded, while monotonous or routine ones will remain unseen or in the background. Jeanne's sex work is accorded no more importance than her housework, and neither is glamorized in any way. Something dramatic does eventually happen (which I won't describe, because it's worth watching this film for yourself), but Akerman resolutely resists treating any part of the narrative, such as it is, in the conventional Hollywood manner.

At the end of her essay Laura Mulvey acknowledged that radical filmmakers like Akerman denied audiences the kind of pleasure and satisfaction they got from conventional narrative cinema. In her opinion that was no great loss: feminists, she suggested, should not lament the decline of a tradition which used images of women to satisfy the desires of men. More than forty years later, though, the tradition Mulvey criticized does not seem to be in decline: most moviegoers are still wedded to the pleasures of narrative cinema. So, while there is nothing wrong with making feminist art that radically challenges audience expectations, there is also an argument for less radical challenges to the sexism of mainstream culture, of the kind proposed by Susanna White—more women behind the camera, more leading and speaking roles for women in front of it, and more diversity in the stories told on film.

I call these less radical challenges, but in recent years it has often seemed as if any kind of feminist challenge is considered intolerably radical. Think, for instance, how much outrage was generated by the 2016 remake of the popular Hollywood film *Ghostbusters*, which cast four women in the lead roles originally played by men. Or think about the prolonged campaign of harassment Anita Sarkeesian was subjected to in 2012 after she made a series of videos analyzing sexist tropes in video games. One of her harassers designed a game called "Beat up Anita Sarkeesian," while another threatened to shoot her at a lecture she was scheduled to deliver. At one point the threats became so numerous and so extreme, she was forced to move out of her home. These responses seem out of all proportion to what precipitated them. Why were so many people so incensed by the idea that there might be room in the world for *one* mainstream movie in which women played all the main roles, or *one* voice criticizing video games?

The intensity of the anger may speak not only to the belief of antifeminists that culture is or should be a male preserve, but also to the centrality of cultural issues in contemporary sexual politics. Some of today's most prominent antifeminist ideologues, the "meninists" of the alt-right, put most of their energy into cultural politics because they believe that culture change leads to political change, rather than vice versa.[20] Feminists too have always understood that the cultural is political: ideas, images, stories, and theories play an important part in challenging inequality, just as they do in maintaining it. But what the alt-right has been able to harness in recent years is the feeling among some men in Western democracies that cultural privilege is the only kind they have left. Though it's easy to mock these men's priorities ("we've let women be astronauts, scientists, and presidential candidates, but NO WAY are we going to let them be ghostbusters!"), the resentment is real, and its consequences are serious. For feminism this is not a new battleground, but we should not underestimate its current and future importance.

7
Fault Lines and Futures

Attempts to summarize the current state of feminism crop up regularly. *Prospect* magazine published one in 2017 with the title "Everything You Wanted to Know about Fourth Wave Feminism—but Were Afraid to Ask." "New breadth," the article said, "has made it harder to define a coherent feminism for the twenty-first century."[1] If "coherent" means unified in ideas and political goals, then it isn't obvious that today's feminism is less coherent than what preceded it; hindsight often makes the past look more coherent than it felt to the people for whom it was the present. But it could be argued that a kind of coherence is now being imposed from the outside, as feminists confront the challenges of the current political situation.

Since the 2008 financial crisis, the situation of women in many places has worsened both economically, because of the impact of government austerity programs, and politically, because of a resurgence of nationalism and right-wing authoritarianism. In diverse countries such as India, Poland, Russia, Turkey, and the United States, authoritarian leaders and conservative lawmakers are making efforts to reverse the gains of the recent past. In Poland they tried to ban abortion completely; in Russia they have decriminalized many forms of domestic violence, and in 2017 Human Rights Watch reported that a group of Russian women attending a feminist event had been interrogated by the police and warned about their "extremist activities."[2] In other places it is far-right groups who are harassing feminists. In the United States, analysts have found a strong connection between involvement in neo-Nazi or white supremacist organizations and engagement in antifeminist men's-rights activism. In these conditions the political agenda becomes all too clear: "fight back." Coherence is not always a good sign.

Effective resistance requires a broad-based coalition in which diverse constituencies and voices are represented. For feminists, that underlines, once again, the necessity of acknowledging and addressing relations of power and inequality among women. In principle this is something they agree on. The *Prospect* article is not the first to suggest that commitment to the principle of intersectionality is one of the defining features of the fourth wave. But it is one thing to talk the intersectional talk, and another to walk the walk. The women's marches that were organized to protest Donald Trump's inauguration were on one level an impressive display of feminist unity, but they were also the site of conflicts about the exclusion or marginalization of some groups of women by others. Black women pointed out that the original organizers were all white, and that the names they chose for the event were borrowed, without acknowledgment, from earlier Black women's and civil rights protests. There was also some debate on whether the signature "pussy hats" and "pussy power" signs (references to the infamous tape on which Trump was heard boasting about "grabbing women by the pussy") were exclusionary and disrespectful to trans women.

This dispute about whether the marches were trans-exclusionary points to another characteristic of the fourth wave: its concern with questions about gender identity and diversity. For most of its history feminism has been understood, and often referred to, as a "women's movement," defined by the political goal of securing equality or liberation for women as a class. To suggest, as the British journalist Laurie Penny did in 2015, that feminism's focus on women can be alienating[3] would in the past have been rather like complaining that a baker's shop sold bread. Today, however, a significant constituency within feminism is questioning the basis for the traditional definition. Penny belongs to a new wave of "genderqueer" activists who conceive of feminism not simply as a movement to end the oppression of women and the dominance of men but as a movement to liberate everyone from the binary gender system that produces these two categories.

Like many other people who define themselves as something other than men or women—trans, nonbinary, agender, genderfluid, genderqueer—Penny recalls feeling from an early age that the standard binary categories were inadequate to capture her own sense of who she was (though she has continued to define herself as a woman and would not object to my use of the pronoun "she"). From this perspective gender is not seen in the way second-wave feminists saw it, as a set of restrictive and unequal roles imposed by societies on their male and female members, but rather as a form of identity that individuals should be free to define for themselves. Whereas second-wave feminists often imagined, both in their political writings and in utopian fiction, a future world without gender distinctions, Penny has a different vision: "I don't want to see a world without gender. I want to see a world where gender is not oppressive or enforced, where there are as many ways to express and perform and relate to your own identity as there are people on Earth. I want a world where gender is not painful, but joyful."[4]

It could be argued that this isn't, in the end, so very

different from what feminists who follow in Firestone's footsteps want to see. If there really were as many gender identities as there were people on the planet, then gender as we have known it would effectively have ceased to exist: the word would no longer refer to a social role imposed on the basis of a person's sex but something more like a set of behaviors that express an individual's unique sense of self. But if Penny's genderqueer feminism and the descendant of Firestone's radical feminism are just different routes to the same destination, why is there a conflict between them?

One answer is that while virtually all feminists agree that gender is socially constructed, they have differing ideas about what it is constructed for, and whose interests it serves for it to be constructed in the ways it is. As I explained in chapter 4, it can be argued that the qualities and behaviors a culture codes as feminine or masculine are not just arbitrarily different but are designed to justify men's dominance while keeping women in their subordinate place. Feminists who see gender in this way are skeptical about the idea that self-conscious or ironic performances of femininity and masculinity are politically subversive.[5] As Penny notes (though she herself does not agree), some feminists feel that queer and trans performances, especially if they involve a stereotypical version of gender, do not subvert but rather reinforce the system that subordinates women to men. Another answer is that contemporary gender-identity politics raises questions about what defines the category "women," and this is also something feminists have differing views on. Though most subscribe to the belief that one is not born a woman, but becomes one, the question can still be asked, How does one become a woman? Can anyone become a woman, or does it require a certain kind of personal history (for instance, of being treated from birth in the way your culture treats girls, as opposed to the way it treats boys)? Are there aspects of becoming a woman that are inextricably linked to having a certain kind of body? Even if we acknowledge that bodies exist in a social context that profoundly shapes the experience of embodiment, are there material bodily realities that will always be relevant to the feminist project of ending women's oppression?

Penny believes that the traditional feminist project and genderqueer feminism are not incompatible; she says that "sex is also a political category, and politically, I'm still on the girls' team."[6] But other feminists (on both sides) are less sure that the two perspectives can be reconciled. This has become a high-profile and very polarized debate, but it is also a fast-moving one; how it will develop even in the short term is hard to predict. The conflict it has generated is often presented as primarily generational: critics of the new gender-identity politics are said to be older feminists whose perspective will inevitably become less relevant as they are gradually outnumbered by younger women. But this may be another case of something I mentioned in the introduction, the tendency of the wave model to flatten out the political differences that exist within each generation of feminists. Different and conflicting views about the nature and meaning of gender go along with differing ideas about what feminism is and what it is for. Those differences run through feminism's history, and there is no reason to think they will not be part of its future.

The prominence of gender identity as an issue in contemporary feminism reflects a more general cultural preoccupation with identity in all its forms, and this has prompted some critical reflections on the current state of feminism. In the twenty-first century, feminism itself has increasingly come to be conceptualized as a kind of personal identity rather than as a political project: we ask, "*Is* person X a feminist?" rather than, "Does person X *do* feminism?" Some commentators have linked the rise of feminism-as-identity to the way consumer capitalism appropriates images and ideas from grassroots movements and makes them into marketable commodities. In her book *We Were Feminists Once*, Andi Zeisler argues that feminism is now being promoted as "an identity that everyone can and should consume," and that the result is to dilute and depoliticize it.[7] People who may have no commitment to any concrete political project are being encouraged to claim a feminist identity simply by purchasing products that symbolize feminism. An example turned up in my Facebook feed: it was an advertisement for a product called FeministBox. The box contained a T-shirt, a tote bag, a button, some stickers, a book, and two zines—plus a coupon for a discount on the company's other products. In 2017 fashion-conscious consumers with enough disposable cash could also consider purchasing, for $710 (with a percentage of the proceeds going to a charity founded by Rihanna), Dior's limited edition T-shirt emblazoned with the words, "We should all be feminists."

Another criticism of this commodified version of feminism is that it reduces political questions to matters of personal choice, producing the sort of vacuous discourse parodied in the satirical newspaper the *Onion*, which once marked International Women's Day with an article entitled "Women Now Empowered by Anything a Woman Does." The attitude this headline satirizes is also one of the targets of Jessa Crispin's polemic *Why I Am Not a Feminist*, one chapter of which is (sarcastically) entitled "Every Option Is Equally Feminist."[8] Crispin's point is that endorsing anything that any woman does as a valid feminist choice is incompatible with the goal of a radical political movement, which is not to make everyone feel comfortable with the status quo but on the contrary, to change it. Yet as she says, feminists who offer a critical analysis of some patriarchal social practice or institution are frequently called out by other feminists for disrespecting women's choices. In 2017, for instance, the novelist Zadie Smith told an audience at the Edinburgh Book Festival that she worried about girls' spending too much time on beauty and makeup routines, adding that she limited her own daughter's mirror time to fifteen minutes a day.[9] This was clearly intended as a criticism of the "beauty demands" I discussed in chapter 4, which have been seen as a problem by feminists since Wollstonecraft. But some feminists accused Smith of attacking women who choose to wear makeup; it was also suggested that she had no business voicing an opinion because she herself was too beautiful to need cosmetic enhancement.

Feminism is currently having one of its periodic moments of being "on trend," but the question raised by writers like Zeisler and Crispin is whether its mainstream appeal depends on watering down its political message and reducing the commitment it entails to a series of symbolic gestures. Both writers emphasize that "real" feminism, the kind that makes a difference politically, is not so easy or undemanding: it requires time, effort, perseverance, and resilience in the face of others' indifference or hostility. But Crispin in particular has been criticized for implying that the kind of feminism she rejects (which she refers to as "universal feminism"; others have called it "liberal" or "lifestyle" feminism) is now the dominant if not the only kind, and for failing to acknowledge the continued existence of more radical currents of feminist thinking and activism. As I have argued throughout this book, feminism has never, at any point in its history, been a single, internally homogeneous entity. It has always come in many varieties, and this has always prompted some feminists to criticize others' politics as insufficiently radical. Crispin's complaint about contemporary feminism is not new. As long ago as 1984, bell hooks wrote that "the ideology of competitive, atomistic liberal individualism has permeated feminist thought to such an extent that it undermines the potential radicalism of feminist struggle."[10]

Lifestyle feminism may be highly visible in contemporary popular culture (not surprisingly, given that popular culture is also consumerist and individualist), but the kind of feminism that requires a deeper political commitment is still very much alive. Instead of lamenting its imagined demise, perhaps we should be asking what has enabled it to persist. What inspires and sustains the commitment of feminists to what Crispin describes as the unfashionable and neglected work of creating a more equal society?

When I put that question to a group of feminist women, their answers focused on the way they felt feminism had enriched their lives. For one thing, it had given them a new understanding of the world: many spoke of the relief they felt when they discovered a community of women who felt the same dissatisfactions they had believed they were alone in feeling, and had a political language in which to articulate those dissatisfactions. "It saved my sanity," said one; another said, "it changed my life." Feminism had also enabled them to form some of their closest and most valued relationships with other women (as one put it, "badass women who are not afraid to think for themselves"). And being involved in feminist politics had reinforced their belief that grassroots activism could make a difference: "feminism offers optimism. It gives the opportunity to create change." Though they had all had to deal with political conflicts and setbacks, they were generally optimistic about the future.

Whatever the challenges facing feminism today, I think this optimism is justified. The basic principles of feminism have achieved global currency; their influence is felt in some way in virtually all contemporary societies, including those that still deny women basic rights and freedoms. Though it will continue to be resisted in some quarters, and to provoke arguments about what follows from it in practice, "the radical notion that women are people" is not going to go away.

Notes

Introduction

1. Chimamanda Ngozi Adichie, *We Should All Be Feminists* (Fourth Estate, 2014).

2. See Kathy Frankovic, "Feminism Today: What Does It Mean?," YouGov, August 1, 2014, https://today.yougov.com/news/2014/08/01/feminism-today-what-does-it-mean/.

3. Dorothy L. Sayers, "Are Women Human?," in *Are Women Human? Penetrating, Sensible, and Witty Essays on the Role of Women in Society* (William B. Eerdmans, 2005), 21.

4. Winifred Holtby, *Women and a Changing Civilisation* (John Lane, 1934), 96.

5. The writer and editor Marie Shear coined this definition. Marie Shear, "Media Watch: Celebrating Women's Words," review of *A Feminist Dictionary*, by Cheris Kramarae and Paula A. Treichler with Ann Russo, *New Directions for Women* 15, no. 3 (May–June 1986): 6, https://voices.revealdigital.com/cgi-bin/independentvoices?a=d&d=DGBHBCA19860601.1.6&e=-------en-20--1--txt-txIN-new+directions+for+women-------------1.

6. bell hooks, *Feminism Is for Everybody: Passionate Politics*, rev. ed. (Routledge, 2015), 1.

7. Nancy Hartsock, "Feminist Theory and the Development of Revolutionary Strategy," in *Capitalist Patriarchy and the Case for Socialist Feminism*, ed. Zillah Eisenstein (Monthly Review Press, 1979), 58.

8. Christine de Pizan, *The Book of the City of Ladies*, trans. Rosalind Brown-Grant (Penguin, 1999).

9. On the relationships between Black and white women in the American suffrage movement, see Angela Davis, *Women, Race and Class* (Vintage, 1983); Paula Giddings, *When and Where I Enter: The Impact of Black Women on Race and Sex in America* (William Morrow, 2007).

10. Two histories of American feminism that discuss its relationships with other political movements are Dorothy Sue Cobble, Linda Gordon, and Astrid Henry, *Feminism Unfinished: A Short, Surprising History of American Women's Movements* (Norton, 2014); Annelise Orleck, *Rethinking American Women's Activism* (Routledge, 2015).

11. Mary Wollstonecraft, *A Vindication of the Rights of Woman* (Vintage, 2015); Simone de Beauvoir, *The Second Sex*, trans. Constance Borde and Sheila Malovany-Chevallier (Knopf, 2009).

12. For Kimberlé Crenshaw's discussion of intersectionality, see Kimberlé Crenshaw, "The Urgency of Intersectionality" (lecture, TED-Women 2016, San Francisco, October 27, 2016), http://www.ted.com /talks/kimberle_crenshaw_the_urgency_of_intersectionality. A (short) book-length introduction to the subject is Patricia Hill Collins and Sirma Bilge, *Intersectionality* (Polity Press, 2016).

13. Cherríe Moraga, preface to *This Bridge Called My Back: Radical Writings by Women of Color*, 4th ed., ed. Cherríe Moraga and Gloria Anzaldúa (SUNY Press, 2015), xvi.

14. For more on the interplay between local and global, see Amrita Basu, ed., *Women's Movements in the Global Era* (Westview Press, 2016), which focuses particularly on women's and feminist movements in the global South.

Chapter One

1. Naomi Alderman, *The Power* (Penguin, 2016).

2. Charlotte Perkins Gilman, *Herland* (Vintage Classics, 2015); Marge Piercy, *Woman on the Edge of Time* (Knopf, 1976). For more on speculative fiction as a vehicle for exploring feminist theoretical ideas, see Judith Little, ed., *Feminist Philosophy and Science Fiction: Utopias and Dystopias* (Prometheus Books, 2007).

3. See Sally G. McMillen, *Lucy Stone: An Unapologetic Life* (Oxford University Press, 2015).

4. Friedrich Engels, *The Origin of the Family, Private Property, and the State*, 4th ed. (Foreign Languages Publishing House, 1891); quote appears on page 30 of https://www.marxists.org/archive/marx/works /download/pdf/origin_family.pdf.

5. Gerda Lerner, *The Creation of Patriarchy* (Oxford University Press, 1986).

6. See Michelle Rosaldo and Louise Lamphere, eds., *Women, Culture and Society* (Stanford University Press, 1974); Rayna R. Reiter, ed., *Toward an Anthropology of Women* (Monthly Review Press, 1975).

7. M. Dyble, G. D. Salali, N. Chaudhary, A. Page, D. Smith, J. Thompson, L. Vinicius, R. Mace, and A. B. Migliano, "Sex Equality Can Explain the Unique Social Structure of Hunter-Gatherer Bands," *Science*, May 15, 2015, 796–98.

8. Sylvia Walby, *Theorizing Patriarchy* (Blackwell, 1990).

9. Shulamith Firestone, *The Dialectic of Sex* (Bantam Books, 1970), 9, 11.

10. Linda Gordon, *The Moral Property of Women: A History of Birth Control Politics in America* (University of Illinois Press, 2002), 320.

11. Susan Sontag, "The Third World of Women," *Partisan Review* 40, no. 2 (1973): 184.

Chapter Two

1. Charlotte Bunch, "Women's Rights as Human Rights: Toward a Re-vision of Human Rights," *Human Rights Quarterly* 12, no. 4 (1990): 486–98; Hillary Rodham Clinton, Remarks to the United Nations Fourth World Conference on Women Plenary Session, Beijing, China, September 5, 1995, http://www.americanrhetoric.com/speeches /hillaryclintonbeijingspeech.htm.

2. Wollstonecraft, *A Vindication*, 24.

3. On Emma Goldman and her relationship to feminism, see Alix Kates Shulman, ed., *Red Emma Speaks* (Open Road Media, 2012); Penny A. Weiss and Loretta Kensinger, *Feminist Interpretations of Emma Goldman* (Pennsylvania State University Press, 2007).

4. This story is told in Gillian Thomas, *Because of Sex: One Law, Ten Cases and Fifty Years That Changed American Women's Lives at Work* (Picador, 2017).

5. See Oren Peleg, "Arkansas Law Allows Father to Veto Abortion," Opposing Views, February 2, 2017, https://www.opposingviews.com /category/new-law-lets-dads-veto-abortions. For a more general critical discussion of antiabortion activism in the United States since *Roe v. Wade*, see Katha Pollitt, *Pro: Reclaiming Abortion Rights* (Picador, 2014).

6. Catharine MacKinnon, *Are Women Human?* (Harvard University Press, 2006).

7. Bunch, "Women's Rights as Human Rights," 186. Bunch also talks about her work for women's/human rights at Makers, http://www .makers.com/charlotte-bunch.

8. UN Women's website, http://www.unwomen.org/en/what-we -do, offers facts, figures, and links to UN documents, including those cited in this chapter.

9. Angela Y. Davis, *Women, Race and Class* (Vintage, 1983), chap. 12.

10. Margaret Sanger, an early campaigner for birth control and one of the founders of Planned Parenthood, became increasingly committed to eugenicist views. See Davis, *Women, Race and Class*; Gordon, *Moral Property*.

11. For a range of perspectives, see Miranda Davies, ed., *Babies for Sale? Transnational Surrogacy, Human Rights and the Politics of Reproduction* (Zed Books, 2017).

12. See Christine Delphy, *Separate and Dominate* (Verso, 2015).

13. See Pragna Patel, "The Sharia Debate in the UK: Who Will Listen to Our Voices?," openDemocracy, December 14, 2016, https://www.opendemocracy.net/5050/pragna-patel/sharia-debate-who-will-listen-to-us.

14. Ayelet Shachar, "Entangled: Family, Religion and Human Rights," in *Human Rights: The Hard Questions*, ed. Cindy Holder and David Reidy (Cambridge University Press, 2013), 115–35.

Chapter Three

1. On the class, race, and sexual politics of paid domestic labor, see Bridget Anderson, *Doing the Dirty Work* (Zed Books, 2000).

2. See Human Rights Watch, "Swept under the Rug: Abuses against Domestic Workers around the World," July 27, 2006, https://www.hrw.org/report/2006/07/27/swept-under-rug/abuses-against-domestic-workers-around-world.

3. Amartya Sen, "More Than 100 Million Women Are Missing," *New York Review of Books*, December 20, 1990, http://www.nybooks.com/articles/1990/12/20/more-than-100-million-women-are-missing/.

4. Gaëlle Ferrant, Luca Maria Pesando, and Keiko Nowacka, *Unpaid Care Work: The Missing Link in the Analysis of Gender Gaps in Labour Outcomes* (OECD Development Centre, December 2014), 1, http://www.oecd.org/dev/development-gender/Unpaid_care_work.pdf.

5. Ibid., 10.

6. Quoted in Josh Hafner, "GOP Official in Utah Resigns after Criticizing Equal Pay for Women," *USA Today*, February 20, 2017, https://www.usatoday.com/story/news/politics/onpolitics/2017/02/20/gop-official-utah-resigns-after-criticizing-equal-pay-bill/98155140/.

7. Barbara Ehrenreich, *Nickel and Dimed* (Granta Books, 2002), investigates the reality of life for women working in low-paid, female-dominated occupations in the United States.

8. Ferrant, Pesando, and Nowacka, *Unpaid Care Work*, 10.

9. On the history and politics of the Wages for Housework movement, see Silvia Federici and Arlen Austin, eds., *Wages for Housework: The New York Committee 1972–1977; History, Theory, Documents* (Autonomedia, 2017).

10. Davis, *Women, Race and Class*, chap. 13.

11. Katrine Marçal, *Who Cooked Adam Smith's Dinner?* (Portobello Books, 2015).

12. Huong Dinh, Lyndall Strazdins, and Jennifer Welsh, "Hour-Glass Ceilings: Work-Hour Thresholds, Gendered Health Inequities," *Social Science and Medicine* 176 (March 2017): 42–51.

13. Christin L. Munsch, "Her Support, His Support: Money, Masculinity and Marital Infidelity," *American Sociological Review* 80, no. 3 (2015): 469–95.

Chapter Four

1. Beauvoir, *Second Sex*, 3.

2. Ibid., 283; the quote matches the more familiar 1953 translation by H. M. Parshley rather than the 2009 translation cited above.

3. Margaret Mead, *Sex and Temperament in Three Primitive Societies* (HarperCollins, 2001).

4. Susan Brownmiller, *Femininity* (Simon & Schuster, 1984), 15.

5. Firestone, *Dialectic*, 11.

6. The evolutionary argument was made by Anya C. Hurlbert and Yazhu Ling, "Biological Components of Sex Differences in Color Preference," *Current Biology* 17, no. 16 (August 21, 2007): R623–25, and critiqued soon afterward by Ben Goldacre, "Pink, Pink, Pink, Pink. Pink Moan," Bad Science, *Guardian*, August 25, 2007, http://www.badscience.net/2007/08/pink-pink-pink-pink-pink-moan/.

7. Cordelia Fine, *Delusions of Gender* (Icon Books, 2010), 197. Fine discusses these studies on pages 197–206.

8. Bronwyn Davies, *Frogs and Snails and Feminist Tales* (Hampton Press, 2002).

9. Fine, *Delusions of Gender*, 203.

10. Davies, *Frogs and Snails and Feminist Tales*.

11. Marianne Grabrucker, *There's a Good Girl: Gender Stereotyping in the First Three Years—A Diary* (Woman's Press, 1988).

12. These parents went on to publish a book: Ros Ball and James Millar, *The Gender Agenda* (Jessica Kingsley Publishers, 2017).

13. In 2016 the family revealed that Storm is a girl. See Jessica Botelho-Urbanski, "Baby Storm Five Years Later: Preschooler on Top of the World," *Star*, July 11, 2016, https://www.thestar.com/news/gta/2016/07/11/baby-storm-five-years-later-preschooler-on-top-of-the-world.html.

14. This research is being carried out by linguists Carmen Fought and Karen Eisenhauer. For an account of its initial findings, see Jeff Guo, "Researchers Have Found a Major Problem with 'The Little Mermaid' and Other Disney Movies," *Washington Post*, January 25, 2016, https://www.washingtonpost.com/news/wonk/wp/2016/01/25/researchers-have-discovered-a-major-problem-with-the-little-mermaid-and-other-disney-movies/?utm_term=.9efc314c59e0.

15. Naomi Wolf, *The Beauty Myth* (Chatto & Windus, 1990), 2.

16. Heather Widdows, *Perfect Me: Beauty as an Ethical Ideal* (Princeton University Press, 2018), 2, 30.

17. Paula C. Morrow, "Physical Attractiveness and Selection Decision Making," *Journal of Management* 16, no. 1 (1990): 45–60.

18. Katarzyna Kościcka, Kamila Czepczor, and Anna Brytek-Matera, "Body Size Attitudes and Body Image Perception among Preschool Children and Their Parents: A Preliminary Study," *Archives of Psychiatry and Psychotherapy* 4 (2016): 28–34.

19. Roxane Gay, *Hunger: A Memoir of (My) Body* (HarperCollins, 2017), 5.

20. On racism in the construction of female beauty and the promotion of beauty products, see Liz Conor, "Dove, Real Beauty and the Racist History of Skin Whitening," The Conversation, October 10, 2017, https://theconversation.com/dove-real-beauty-and-the-racist-history -of-skin-whitening-85446.

21. Julia Serano, *Whipping Girl* (Seal Press, 2007).

Chapter Five

1. E. L. James, *Fifty Shades of Grey* (Vintage, 2012).

2. These online comments are quoted in Lisa Downing, "Safewording! Kinkphobia and Gender Normativity in *Fifty Shades of Grey*," *Psychology and Sexuality* 4, no. 1 (2013): 92–102, https://doi.org/10.1080 /19419899.2012.740067.

3. Carole Vance, "Pleasure and Danger: Toward a Politics of Sexuality," in *Pleasure and Danger*, ed. Carole Vance (Routledge, 1984), 1.

4. See Lucy Bland, *Banishing the Beast: Feminism, Sex and Morality* (I. B. Tauris, 2001).

5. Lynne Segal, *Straight Sex: Rethinking the Politics of Pleasure* (Verso, 2015), xii.

6. Anne Koedt, "The Myth of the Vaginal Orgasm," *Notes from the Second Year* (1970), https://wgs10016.commons.gc.cuny.edu/the-myth -of-the-vaginal-orgasm-by-anne-koedt-1970/.

7. According to the Guttmacher Institute's review of states' policies, thirty-seven of fifty states require that school sex-education programs (where provided—only about half of all states mandate them) include instruction on abstinence, and twenty-six of those require that abstinence be "stressed." Guttmacher Institute, *Sex and HIV Education* (June 11, 2018), https://www.guttmacher.org/state-policy/explore/sex-and-hiv -education. The *New York Times* has reported that by 2014, half of all middle schools and more than three-quarters of all high schools were focusing on abstinence. Aaron E. Carroll, "Sex Education Based on Abstinence? There's a Real Absence of Evidence," *New York Times*, August 22, 2017, https://www.nytimes.com/2017/08/22/upshot/sex-education -based-on-abstinence-theres-a-real-absence-of-evidence.html.

8. Peggy Orenstein, *Girls and Sex* (HarperCollins, 2016).

9. See Joseph Price, Rich Patterson, Mark Regnerus, and Jacob Walley, "How Much More XXX Is Generation X Consuming? Evidence of Changing Attitudes and Behaviors Relating to Pornography since 1973," *Journal of Sex Research* 53, no. 1 (2016): 12–20; Tori Deangelis, "Web Pornography's Effect on Children," *Monitor on Psychology* 38, no. 10 (2007): 50.

10. The mainstreaming of porn or "raunch" culture is discussed in Ariel Levy, *Female Chauvinist Pigs* (Pocket Books, 2006).

11. For an examination of the phenomenon of rape culture, see Kate Harding, *Asking for It* (Da Capo Press, 2015).

12. Lisa Downing, "What Is 'Sex Critical' and Why Should We Care about It?," *Sex Critical* (blog), July 27, 2012, http://sexcritical.co.uk/2012 /07/27/what-is-sex-critical-and-why-should-we-care-about-it/.

13. Ruth Rosen, *A Lost Sisterhood: Prostitution in America, 1900–1918* (Johns Hopkins University Press, 1983), xiii.

14. For more on the campaign against the Contagious Diseases Acts in Britain, see Judith Walkowitz, *Prostitution and Victorian Society: Women, Class, and the State* (Cambridge University Press, 1980).

15. The next section gives a condensed account of the competing feminist arguments on prostitution and sex work. For more detail on the "abolitionist," pro–Nordic model position, see Kat Banyard, *Pimp State* (Faber & Faber, 2016). For the opposing arguments, see Laurie Penny, *Meat Market* (Zero Books, 2011).

16. Banyard, *Pimp State*, 69–70.

17. An accessible source of information on the men's rights movement is David Futrelle's website We Hunted the Mammoth, http://www .wehuntedthemammoth.com/. There is also a chapter devoted to the subject in Angela Nagle, *Kill All Normies* (Zero Books, 2017), a history and analysis of the alt-right.

18. A Southern Women's Writing Collective, "Sex Resistance in Heterosexual Arrangements," in *The Sexual Liberals and the Attack on Feminism*, ed. Dorchen Leidholt and Janice G. Richmond (Teachers College Press, 1990), 141, http://www.mediafire.com/file/z55yyg8z1b244ua/Sex +Resistance+in+Heterosexual+Arrangements+-+WAS.pdf.

19. Monique Wittig, "One Is Not Born a Woman," in *The Straight Mind, and Other Essays* (Beacon Press, 1992), 9–20.

20. Adrienne Rich, "Compulsory Heterosexuality and Lesbian Existence," *Signs* 5, no. 4, special issue, *Women: Sex and Sexuality* (Summer 1980): 631–60; reprinted in *Journal of Women's History* 15, no. 3 (Autumn 2003): 11–48.

21. Friedan's comment, and the response it provoked from lesbian feminists, is discussed in Karla Jay, *Tales of the Lavender Menace: A Memoir of Liberation* (Basic Books, 2000), 137–47.

22. The Combahee River Collective Statement is an important document in Black and LGBT as well as feminist history, and it has been reprinted in numerous sources, including a collection edited by one of the collective's founders. See Barbara Smith, ed., *Home Girls: A Black Feminist Anthology* (Rutgers University Press, 2000), 264–74. The full text is also available online at http://circuitous.org/scraps/combahee .html.

23. Smith, *Home Girls*, 264.

24. Christina Cauterucci, "For Many Young, Queer Women, *Lesbian* Offers a Fraught Inheritance," *Outward* (blog), *Slate*, December 20, 2016, http://www.slate.com/blogs/outward/2016/12/20/young_queer _women_don_t_like_lesbian_as_a_name_here_s_why.html.

25. Shannon Keating, "Can Lesbian Identity Survive the Gender Revolution?," *BuzzFeed*, February 11, 2017, https://www.buzzfeed.com /shannonkeating/can-lesbian-identity-survive-the-gender-revolution ?utm_term=.jk4oPA6kP#.ouLrk3awk.

Chapter Six

1. Camille Paglia, *Sexual Personae: Art and Decadence from Nefertiti to Emily Dickinson* (Vintage, 1991), 38.

2. Charles Darwin, *The Descent of Man, and Selection in Relation to Sex* (J. Murray, 1871); repr., Charles Darwin, *Evolutionary Writings*, ed. John Secord (Oxford University Press, 2008), 304.

3. Cesare Lombroso, *The Man of Genius* (CreateSpace Independent Publishing Platform, 2015), 123–24. Lombroso credited the writer and critic Edmond de Goncourt with the comment about women of genius but did not specify the source of that observation. Ibid., 124.

4. Antoinette Brown Blackwell, *The Sexes throughout Nature* (Putnam, 1875).

5. Virginia Woolf, *A Room of One's Own* (Penguin Modern Classics, 2002).

6. Alice Walker, "In Search of Our Mothers' Gardens," in *In Search of Our Mothers' Gardens: Womanist Prose* (Mariner Books, 2004), 233. The text of the essay can also be read online at http://www.msmagazine .com/spring2002/walker.asp.

7. Susanna White, "A Screen of One's Own" (lecture, Exeter College, University of Oxford, Oxford, UK, March 6, 2017), https://www .directors.uk.com/news/a-screen-of-one-s-own-a-fulbright-lecture-by -susanna-white.

8. Firestone, *Dialectic*, 157.

9. Anna Beer, *Sounds and Sweet Airs: The Forgotten Women of Classical Music* (Oneworld Publications, 2016).

10. Mary Ellmann, *Thinking about Women* (Harcourt, 1968), 29.

11. Catherine Nichols, "Homme de Plume: What I Learned Sending My Novel Out under a Male Name," *Jezebel* (blog), August 4, 2015, https://jezebel.com/homme-de-plume-what-i-learned-sending-my-novel-out-und-1720637627.

12. Lili Loofbourow, "The Male Glance," *Virginia Quarterly Review* 94, no. 1 (Spring 2018), https://www.vqronline.org/essays-articles/2018/03/male-glance.

13. Beauvoir, *Second Sex*, 162.

14. Firestone, *Dialectic*, 159.

15. John Berger, *Ways of Seeing* (Penguin, 1972), 47. The relevant episode of the TV series can be viewed at https://www.youtube.com/watch?v=m1GI8mNU5Sg.

16. Berger, *Ways of Seeing*, 51.

17. This essay appears in many anthologies, but the original version is Laura Mulvey, "Visual Pleasure and Narrative Cinema," *Screen* 16, no. 3 (Autumn 1975): 6–18.

18. On racism and the representation of Black women, see bell hooks, *Black Looks: Race and Representation*, rev. ed. (Routledge, 2015).

19. T. Denean Sharpley-Whiting, *Black Venus* (Duke University Press, 1999), 17.

20. See Nagle, *Kill All Normies*, for more discussion of the alt-right's approach to cultural politics.

Chapter Seven

1. Jessica Abrahams, "Everything You Wanted to Know about Fourth Wave Feminism—but Were Afraid to Ask," *Prospect*, September 2017, https://www.prospectmagazine.co.uk/magazine/everything-wanted-know-fourth-wave-feminism.

2. See Jason La Miere, "Russia Now Treating Feminists as 'Extremists' as Putin Continues Crackdown," *Newsweek*, August 16, 2017, http://www.newsweek.com/russia-extremism-feminism-putin-jehovah-651168.

3. Laurie Penny, "How to Be a Genderqueer Feminist," *BuzzFeed*, October 31, 2015, https://www.buzzfeed.com/lauriepenny/how-to-be-a-genderqueer-feminist.

4. Ibid.

5. An influential theoretical source for arguments about the politics of performing gender is Judith Butler, *Gender Trouble: Feminism and the Subversion of Identity* (Routledge, 1990).

6. Penny, "How to Be a Genderqueer Feminist."

7. Andi Zeisler, *We Were Feminists Once* (PublicAffairs, 2016), 74.

8. Jessa Crispin, *Why I Am Not a Feminist: A Feminist Manifesto* (Melville House, 2017).

9. See David Sanderson, "Girls Are Fools to Waste Time on Beauty, Says Zadie Smith," *Times*, August 21, 2017, https://www.thetimes.co .uk/article/girls-are-fools-to-waste-time-on-beauty-says-zadiesmith -pd9jhzzbb.

10. bell hooks, *Feminist Theory: From Margin to Center* (South End Press, 1984), 9.

Index